CONTENTS

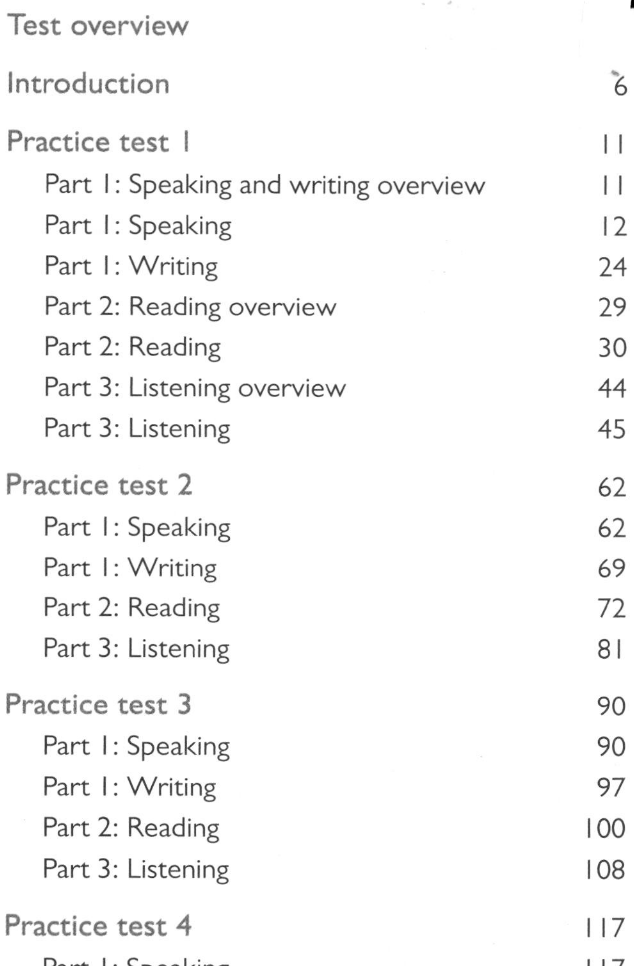

INTRODUCTION

Test overview

PTE Academic (Pearson Test of English Academic) is an international computer-based English language test. It accurately measures English language ability and can be used to apply to educational institutions, and professional and government organizations. The test uses task-based questions to represent the kinds of functions and situations students will find themselves in during academic study.

Most real-life tasks in an academic setting involve using more than one language skill together, for example listening to a lecture and writing notes. PTE Academic reflects this through its 20 task types, each of which tests a combination of skills. For example, one task type asks you to demonstrate your understanding of a passage by providing a written summary, while another tests your understanding of a lecture by asking you to re-tell the lecture.

The test is divided into three main parts and lasts for approximately three hours with an optional break of ten minutes:

Part 1: Speaking and writing (77–93 minutes)

Part 2: Reading (32–41 minutes)

Part 3: Listening (45–57 minutes)

Part 1: Speaking and writing

Section	Task type	Task description	Time allowed
Section 1	Personal introduction	After reading the instructions, you have 30 seconds to give a recorded introduction about yourself. This part is not assessed, but is sent to institutions you choose along with your Score Report.	1 minute
Section 2	Read aloud	A text appears on screen. Read the text aloud.	30–35 minutes
	Repeat sentence	After listening to a sentence, repeat the sentence.	
	Describe image	An image appears on screen. Describe the image in detail.	
	Re-tell lecture	After listening to or watching a video of a lecture, re-tell the lecture in your own words.	
	Answer short question	After listening to a question, answer with a single word or a few words.	
Section 3–4	Summarize written text	After reading a passage, write a one-sentence summary of the passage of between 5 and 75 words.	20 minutes
Section 5	Summarize written text or Write essay	Either a *Summarize written text* task or a *Write essay* task, depending on the combination of tasks in your test.	10 or 20 minutes
Section 6	Write essay	Write an essay of 200–300 words on a given topic.	20 minutes

For more detail, see the Speaking and writing overview on page 11.

Part 2: Reading

Section	Task type	Task description	Time allowed
	Multiple-choice, choose single answer	After reading a text, answer a multiple-choice question on the content or tone of the text by selecting one response.	32–41 minutes
	Multiple-choice, choose multiple answers	After reading a text, answer a multiple-choice question on the content or tone of the text by selecting more than one response.	
	Re-order paragraphs	Several text boxes appear on screen in random order. Put the text boxes in the correct order.	
	Reading: Fill in the blanks	A text appears on screen with several blanks. Drag words or phrases from the blue box to fill in the blanks.	
	Reading & writing: Fill in the blanks	A text appears on screen with several blanks. Fill in the blanks by selecting words from several drop-down lists of response options.	

For more detail, see the Reading overview on page 29.

Part 3: Listening

Section	Task type	Task description	Time allowed
Section 1	Summarize spoken text	After listening to a recording, write a summary of 50–70 words.	20 or 30 minutes
Section 2	Multiple-choice, choose multiple answers	After listening to a recording, answer a multiple-choice question on the content or tone of the recording by selecting more than one response.	23–28 minutes
	Fill in the blanks	The transcription of a recording appears on screen with several blanks. While listening to the recording, type the missing words into the blanks.	
	Highlight correct summary	After listening to a recording, select the paragraph that best summarizes the recording.	
	Multiple-choice, choose single answer	After listening to a recording, answer a multiple-choice question on the content or tone of the recording by selecting one response.	
	Select missing word	After listening to a recording, select the missing word or group of words that completes the recording.	
	Highlight incorrect words	The transcription of a recording appears on screen. While listening to the recording, identify the words in the transcription that differ from what is said.	
	Write from dictation	After listening to a recording of a sentence, type the sentence.	

For more detail, see the Listening overview on page 44.

Introduction to PTE Academic Practice Tests Plus

PTE Academic Practice Tests Plus includes three main sections

First, there is an introduction to the test and to the *Practice Tests Plus* book. This gives you information about the test itself, about taking the test, and about how you can use this book to help you prepare.

The main section of the book is the practice tests. There are four complete tests, all written by people who write the actual test. Test 1 provides a full page of information and strategies for each of the 20 task types. There is a tip for each question in Test 1 to help you get used to the task and how to approach it. Some tips refer directly to the content of the question and some give general guidance. In Test 2, there is one tip for each task type with a useful reminder of how to do the task. Then, in Tests 3 and 4, you're on your own!

Finally, the *with key* version of the book includes the detailed answer key, audio scripts and sample answers from PTE Academic students along with explanations to help you see how your answers might score.

Paper-based practice – computer-based test

You will do the actual test on a computer at a Pearson test centre and when you complete a task, the next one will appear on the screen. You will hear the audio through your headphones and speak into the microphone on your headset. You will be able to take notes on an Erasable Noteboard Booklet, but you will type your answers into the computer.

The practice tests in this book are paper-based and are designed to be used in class or for self study. The instructions on the page are exactly the same as those you will get in the actual test. This means you won't have any surprises when you get to the test centre! However, because the instructions are for a digital format, they don't tell you exactly what to do on paper. You will find some advice on this below.

You can see what the task will look like on screen in Test 1, where you will find a screenshot for each task type in the *About the task type* section before the actual tasks. You will also find a grey 'In the test' box with a mouse cursor at the beginning of each task type in all four tests. This gives you a short description of the on-screen task.

In the test, there are 6–7 tasks. For each task, you read the text aloud into the microphone. The wording in the instructions below is the same as you will see in the actual test. See page 12 for help.

Timings

In the test, some tasks are automatically timed by the length of the audio and some tasks have a timer. When you use the *Practice Tests Plus* book, you can choose to time yourself or to take as long as you need. You could time yourself using your watch, mobile phone or computer.

If there is a time limit for a task, you will find this information in the timer icon next to the instructions.

Listening tasks

For some tasks, you have to listen to an audio extract and then complete the task. In the test, the audio will begin automatically after you have had time to read the instructions. Using the practice tests, you will have to play the relevant audio track yourself. You will find the relevant track number next to the task. 1 ▶31

Each task is on a separate track. This means you can work on tasks individually, or keep the audio running to try a complete set of tasks for a task type.

Giving answers

You will have to give one of three kinds of answers: spoken, written or computer-based interaction (choosing answers from those presented on screen).

Spoken answers

In the test, you will speak into the microphone on your headset. There will be a message on screen telling you when you will begin speaking, and then how long you have been speaking for.

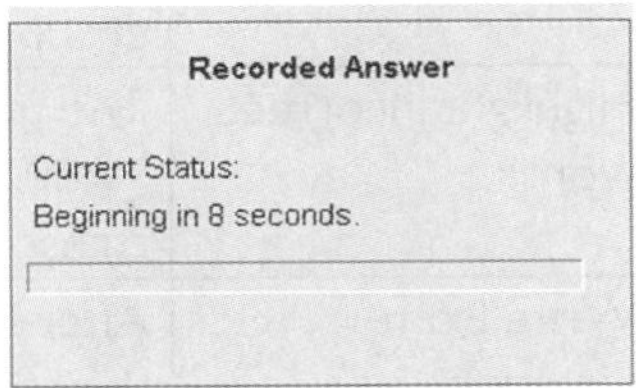

When using the practice tests, it is a good idea to record your answers so that you can listen back and think about how to improve. You could record your answers on your computer or mobile phone. Alternatively, you can work with a partner and take turns to answer the tasks and listen to each other.

Written answers

When you sit the actual test, you will type your answers into the computer. Here, there is space for you to write most of your answers directly into the practice tests book. If you prefer, you could write your answers in a notebook. For the *Write essay* task, it is a good idea to practise typing your answer on the computer. In the test, you will be able to cut, copy and paste text.

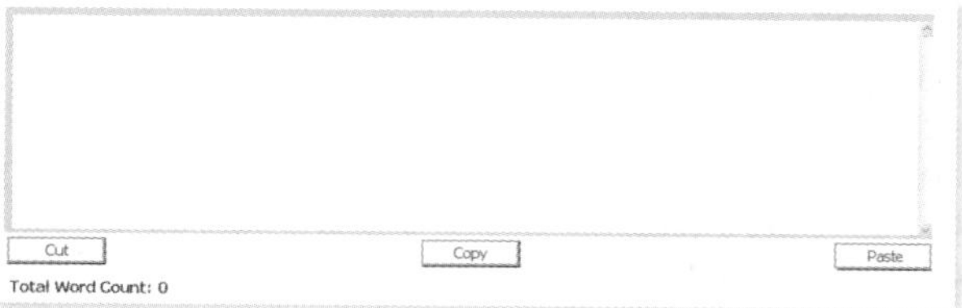

Computer-based interaction

For some tasks in the Reading and Listening parts, you have to use tools on the computer screen, for example click the correct answer from a drop-down list, select the correct button or drag and drop the correct word into the box. Although this book has paper-based practice tests, the instructions are exactly the same as you will see on the computer in the actual test. When practising, simply write your answer in the relevant box, or tick the button next to the correct answer.

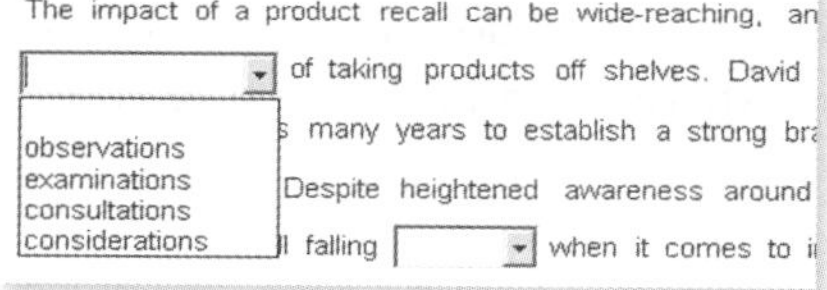

On screen, click the correct answer.

adults' and 'established adults'. [4] [ ] markets no longer talk about 'children', but tend to refer to a fuller range of categories that includes 'kids', 'tweens', 'pre-teens' and 'teenagers'. We now have a very diverse population in terms of age, and that can only be a [5] [*bonus*] for business.

1	A usual	B precise	C right	D honest
2	A linked	B mixed	C concerned	D involved
3	A rather than	B by	C even when	D while
4	A While	B Similarly	C Even	D Really
5	A desire	B favour	C bonus	D promise

On the page, write the correct answer in the box.

Scoring the practice tests

Some tasks in PTE Academic have clear right answers, for example the *Multiple-choice* and *Fill in the blanks* tasks. For these tasks, there are clear answers in the *with key* version of the book.

For most tasks with spoken or written answers, you will score within a range because the task tests a number of language areas, for example content, grammar, etc. For these tasks, you will find three sample responses in the *with key* version of the book, at B1, B2 and C1 level, all with brief explanations. To get an idea of your score on these tasks, look at all of the sample answers. Which is closest to your answer? What did you do better or less well than this student? For the *Write essay* questions, there is also a model essay outline for each task.

Task type	Skills assessed	Type of answer
Part 1: Speaking and writing		
Personal introduction	not assessed	no answer
Read aloud	reading and speaking	sample response
Repeat sentence	listening and speaking	sample response
Describe image	speaking	sample response
Re-tell lecture	listening and speaking	sample response
Answer short question	listening and speaking	right answer
Summarize written text	reading and writing	sample response
Write essay	writing	sample response
Part 2: Reading		
Multiple-choice, choose single answer	reading	right answer
Multiple-choice, choose multiple answers	reading	right answer
Re-order paragraphs	reading	right answer
Reading: Fill in the blanks	reading	right answer
Reading & writing: Fill in the blanks	reading and writing	right answer
Part 3: Listening		
Summarize spoken text	listening and writing	sample response
Multiple-choice, choose multiple answers	listening	right answer
Fill in the blanks	listening and writing	right answer
Highlight correct summary	listening and reading	right answer
Multiple-choice, choose single answer	listening	right answer
Select missing word	listening	right answer
Highlight incorrect words	listening and reading	right answer
Write from dictation	listening and writing	right answer

Preparing for PTE Academic

If you know exactly what to expect before you sit the test, you will feel more confident on the day and increase your chances of doing well. Try to familiarize yourself with the test as much as possible, for example:

- how long the test lasts, and how this is divided into the different test parts and tasks
- how many tasks there are in each part and in the test as a whole
- what the different task types are
- what you will be asked to do for each task type
- what the tasks will look like on screen
- what skills are assessed in each task type and how they will be scored

Don't forget to think about your personal introduction. See page 10 for more information.

There are many different ways to use the practice tests in this book. You may use them in class or for self study. If you use them in class, your teacher will tell you which sections to complete when and advise you on how to give your answers.

Below you will find some ideas for using the tests for self study.

Get to know the task types

Use Test 1 to focus on the task types, one task type at a time.

- First, read the strategy page to find out what the task involves and what is expected of you. This will also give you some ideas of the kinds of study you need to do to be successful in this task type.
- Next, look at the first task and make sure you understand exactly what you have to do. Use the tip to help you.
- Complete the task as well as you can.
- If you have the *with key* version of the book, look at the score guide at the back of the book and think about what the purpose of the task is. Then look at the key or the sample student answers to get an idea of how you did.
- Work through the rest of the questions for that task type in Test 1.

Think about timing

You could use one of the practice tests to work on timing.

- Look at the instructions or the overview in Test 1 to find out how long you have to answer each task for that task type.
- Think about how you will spend that time. For example, in the *Write essay* task, how much of that time will you spend planning, writing and checking? In the *Describe image* task, how long should you spend on an introductory description, how long on detail and how long on conclusions?
- Set a countdown on your mobile phone or computer, then try one task and get a feel for how long you have to speak, read or write.
- Time yourself, moving immediately on to the next task, and work through all of the tasks for that task type.

Take a mock test

Before you take the actual test, you could work through a whole practice test, timing yourself for each section to get an idea of how you would do on test day. In this case, try to find somewhere quiet and make sure you will not be interrupted.

Analyze your answers

However you have answered the tasks, it is very useful to spend time looking at your answers.

For questions with a spoken response, record yourself completing the tasks. Then think about what you think a good answer would include. If you have the *with key* version, listen to the sample student answers and look at the examiner comments. Then listen to your answer and think about how you did on that task, and how you could improve in the future. Use the score guide to help you.

Similarly, if you need to give a written answer, complete the task. Then look at the answer key, where you will see a model answer with an explanation, where relevant. Look at the sample student answers with comments, and compare them to the model answer and your own. How did you do, and how could you improve in the future?

Taking the test

When you take the actual test, you'll go to one of Pearson's secure test centres. You can find your nearest centre on the Pearson website at www.pearsonpte.com. This is also where you can register and book a test for a time that suits you.

On the day, make sure you arrive early so that you have time to register and go through the security procedure. Then you'll be taken to a computer and the test will begin. All parts of the test are done at a computer and the whole test takes around three hours. This includes an untimed introduction and one optional break of up to ten minutes.

After the test, you'll get an email to tell you that your PTE Academic scores are ready. This is normally within five working days from your test date. You can then log in to your account to view and print your scores, and send them to the institutions that you choose. Your scores are valid for two years from your test date.

Your Score Report

Your Score Report will give you an overall score on the Pearson Scale of English. This will then be broken down into the four communicative skills: listening, reading, speaking and writing. You will also get a score for enabling skills: grammar, oral fluency, pronunciation, spelling, vocabulary and written discourse. Please see page 145 for more detail on scores.

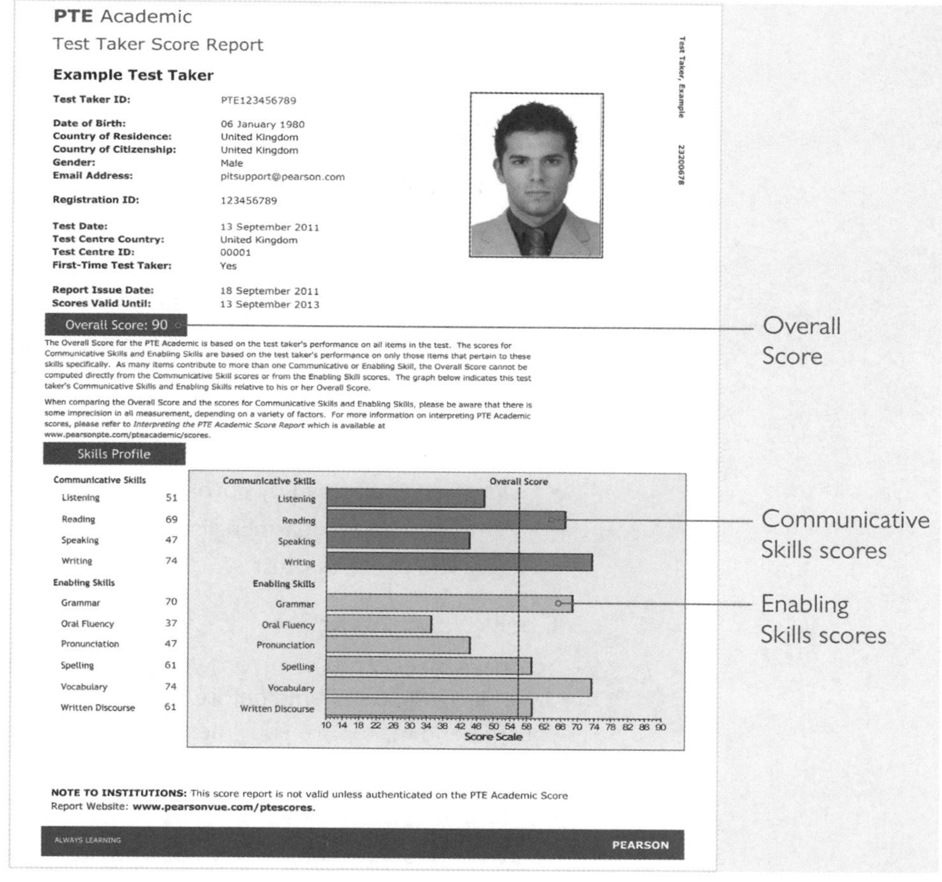

PTE Academic

Test Taker Score Report

Example Test Taker

Test Taker, Example 23200678

Test Taker ID:	PTE123456789
Date of Birth:	06 January 1980
Country of Residence:	United Kingdom
Country of Citizenship:	United Kingdom
Gender:	Male
Email Address:	ptsupport@pearson.com
Registration ID:	123456789
Test Date:	13 September 2011
Test Centre Country:	United Kingdom
Test Centre ID:	00001
First-Time Test Taker:	Yes
Report Issue Date:	18 September 2011
Scores Valid Until:	13 September 2013

Overall Score: 90

The Overall Score for the PTE Academic is based on the test taker's performance on all items in the test. The scores for Communicative Skills and Enabling Skills are based on the test taker's performance on only those items that pertain to these skills specifically. As many items contribute to more than one Communicative or Enabling Skill, the Overall Score cannot be computed directly from the Communicative Skill scores or from the Enabling Skill scores. The graph below indicates this test taker's Communicative Skills and Enabling Skills relative to his or her Overall Score.

When comparing the Overall Score and the scores for Communicative Skills and Enabling Skills, please be aware that there is some imprecision in all measurement, depending on a variety of factors. For more information on interpreting PTE Academic scores, please refer to *Interpreting the PTE Academic Score Report* which is available at www.pearsonpte.com/pteacademic/scores.

Skills Profile

Communicative Skills	
Listening	51
Reading	69
Speaking	47
Writing	74
Enabling Skills	
Grammar	70
Oral Fluency	37
Pronunciation	47
Spelling	61
Vocabulary	74
Written Discourse	61

NOTE TO INSTITUTIONS: This score report is not valid unless authenticated on the PTE Academic Score Report Website: **www.pearsonvue.com/ptescores.**

ALWAYS LEARNING PEARSON

Your Score Report will be ready within five working days.

INTRODUCTION

Personal introduction

About the task type

At the beginning of the test you will be asked to introduce yourself, speaking into the microphone for 30 seconds. This *Personal introduction* is not scored. The purpose is to give university admissions officers an impression of you as a person. Institutions also use the recorded introduction as an additional identity check. Your introduction will be sent along with your Score Report to the institutions that you choose.

You will have 25 seconds to read the instructions, then 30 seconds to record your introduction. There is a Recording Status box which will tell you when to start recording and how much time you have left. You cannot re-record your introduction.

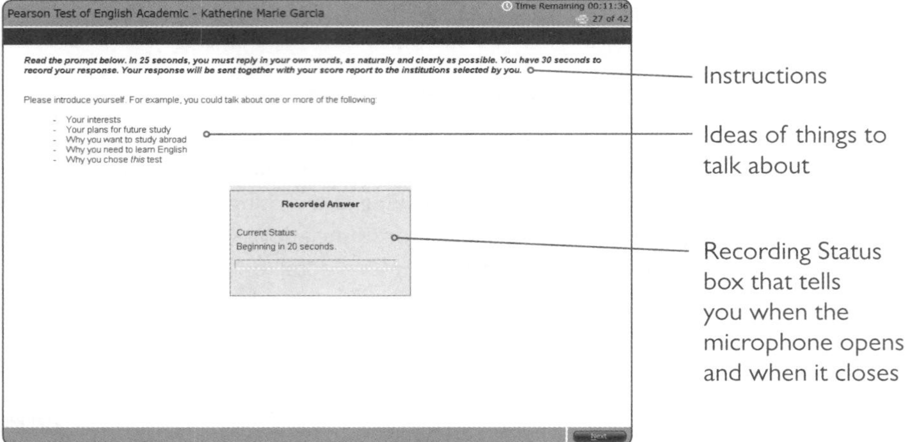

Task strategies

Be prepared!

This is your opportunity to give the admissions officers a first impression of who you are – so make it a positive one! For this task, you can be completely prepared.

Plan in advance what you want to talk about. Start by giving your name, and saying where you're from. Then, include some of the ideas from the instructions:

- Your interests
- Your plans for future study
- Why you want to study abroad
- Why you need to learn English
- Why you chose *this* test

Check your timing

You have 30 seconds to record your message, and you only have one opportunity to get it right! Spend time before the test practising your introduction. Time yourself and make sure your message takes as close to 30 seconds as possible – you don't want to run out of time!

Be yourself

You want to sound natural. Try not to write a speech and memorize it – this can often sound very unnatural and nerves on the day might make you forget the exact words you rehearsed. Instead, practise the kinds of things you want to say. Record yourself speaking, then listen to your introduction. If you were an admissions officer, would your message make a positive impression?

TEST 1

Overview: Speaking and writing

Part 1 of the PTE Academic test is Speaking and writing. This part tests your ability to produce spoken and written English in an academic environment.

The table shows what you will see in the test, which you will take on a computer. When practising with this book, you will have to write your written answers in the book, your notebook or on your own computer, and you could record your spoken answers on your own computer or mobile phone.

Part 1: Speaking and writing					
Speaking (total time 30–35 minutes)					
Task type	**Number of tasks**	**Task description**	**Skills assessed**	**Text/ Recording length**	**Time to answer**
Read aloud	6–7	A text appears on screen. Read the text aloud into your microphone.	reading and speaking	text up to 60 words	varies by task, depending on the length of text
Repeat sentence	10–12	After listening to a sentence, repeat the sentence into your microphone.	listening and speaking	3–9 seconds	15 seconds
Describe image	6–7	An image appears on screen. Describe the image in detail into your microphone.	speaking	n/a	40 seconds
Re-tell lecture	3–4	After listening to or watching a lecture, re-tell the lecture in your own words into your microphone.	listening and speaking	up to 90 seconds	40 seconds
Answer short question	10–12	After listening to a question, answer with a single word or a few words into your microphone.	listening and speaking	3–9 seconds	10 seconds
Writing (total time 50–60 minutes)					
Task type	**Number of tasks**	**Task description**	**Skills assessed**	**Text/ Recording length**	**Time to answer**
Summarize written text	2–3	After reading a passage, write a one-sentence summary of the passage.	reading and writing	text up to 300 words	10 minutes
Write essay	1–2	Write an essay of 200–300 words on a given topic.	writing	up to 4 sentences	20 minutes

Each recording is played only once. You may take notes using the Erasable Noteboard Booklet and pen, and use these notes as a guide when answering the tasks.

Speaking task types are not timed individually, but writing task types are. In both sections you can refer to the timer in the upper right-hand corner of the computer screen, *Time Remaining*, which counts down the time remaining for the Speaking section.

Read aloud

About the task type

This is a long-answer speaking task type that tests reading and speaking skills. You have to read aloud a short text, with correct pronunciation and intonation. You will do 6–7 *Read aloud* tasks.

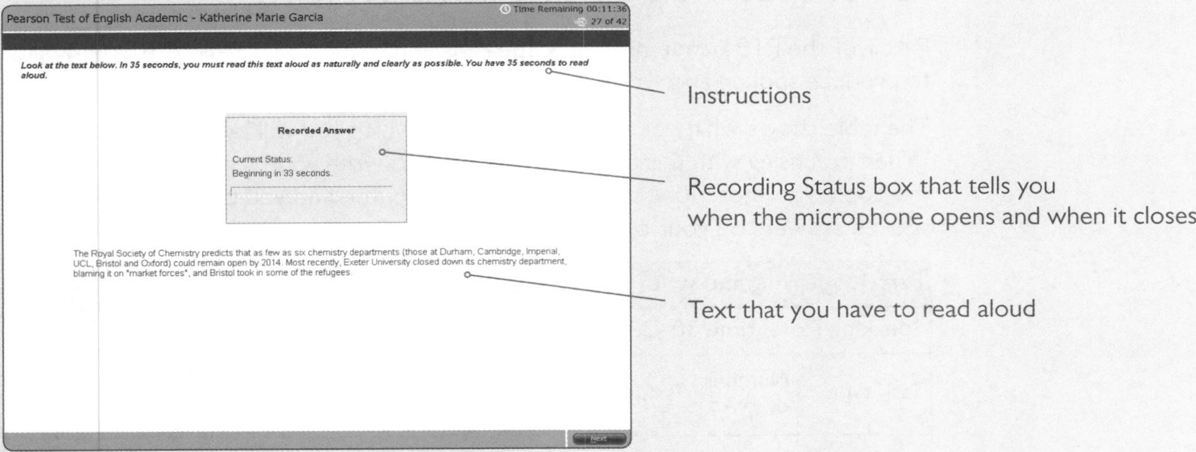

Strategies

Read the text through first

- Use the 30–40 seconds before the microphone opens to skim the text and understand the topic.
- Use the punctuation and grammar to identify where pauses will be needed between meaning groups.
- Identify any words that may be less familiar to you and think how they might be pronounced.
- Read the first part aloud before the microphone opens. This will help you to begin speaking when you hear the tone.

While you read

- Begin reading as soon as the tone sounds and the recording status changes to a blue bar. As you read, stress the words that carry important information. Use pausing to group the text into meaningful chunks.
- Use rising intonation to show a contrast, and falling intonation to show that you have finished a point or sentence, or come to the end of what you are saying.

Take your time

- You have plenty of time so do not rush. Read with meaning, at a normal volume. Do not leave out any words.
- If you make a mistake, correct it and continue. Do not stop reading, and do not begin again at the beginning. Click 'Next' when you are ready to go on to the next task.

Testing focus Scoring ➤ page 147

Subskills tested

Reading: identifying a writer's purpose, style, tone or attitude; understanding academic vocabulary; reading a text under timed conditions.

Speaking: speaking for a purpose (to repeat, to inform, to explain); reading a text aloud; speaking at a natural rate; producing fluent speech; using correct intonation; using correct pronunciation; using correct stress; speaking under timed conditions.

Preparation

- Practise reading sentences out loud, grouping the words into meaningful chunks. Practise putting short pauses at commas and between meaning groups, and longer pauses at full stops.
- Select 6 or 7 short texts of 2 or 3 sentences (up to 60 words) from a magazine or online. Look at the punctuation and grammar and mark the chunks with a slash /. Time yourself reading each one. After 40 seconds, go on to the next text.
- Listen to the way the final sound in one word links to the first sound in the next when people speak. Try to do this when you read aloud.
- You will score higher if your fluency shows a natural rhythm, which is given by chunking and stress. Read a sentence and clap your hands on each stressed word. Be aware of the weak forms between stressed words.
- When practising reading aloud, read on smoothly even if you make a mistake as hesitations, false starts and repetitions can lower your score.
- Practise using rising intonation in lists and falling intonation at the end of sentences.
- When you learn a new word, use a dictionary that has the words recorded so you can check both the pronunciation of the sounds and where the word stress falls.
- You will read more fluently if you understand what you are reading, so work on your reading and vocabulary skills as well as your speaking skills.

Read aloud

TIP STRIP

1. Break the text up into chunks and pause slightly between each one as you read. Before the recording begins, use the punctuation to help you decide where to pause and where each new chunk will begin.
2. As you read, stress the words that carry important information. This makes it easier to understand what you are saying.
3. Use rising intonation patterns to show a contrast. For example, here you need to contrast the *buildings* with *trees*.
4. Try to get the word stress right on multi-syllable words. In Text 4, there are words that end in '*ion*'. Usually, the stress falls on the syllable before this – *pollution*, *combustion*, *stations*.
5. Look for sense groups, as well as the grammatical structure, to notice which groups of words should be said in one chunk: */ to provide individuals with an income / once they stop working /*.
6. Use falling intonation patterns to show that you have finished a point, or come to the end of what you are saying: *on our moods*, *about our lives*.

In the test, there are 6–7 tasks. For each task, you read the text aloud into the microphone. The wording in the instructions below is the same as you will see in the actual test. See page 12 for help.

40 sec. **Look at the text below. In 40 seconds, you must read this text aloud as naturally and as clearly as possible. You have 40 seconds to read aloud.**

1. Market research is a vital part of the planning of any business. However experienced you or your staff may be in a particular field, if you are thinking of introducing a service to a new area, it is important to find out what the local population thinks about it first.

2. Not a lot is known about how the transportation of goods by water first began. Large cargo boats were being used in some parts of the world up to five thousand years ago. However, sea trade became more widespread when large sailing boats travelled between ports, carrying spices, perfumes and objects made by hand.

3. When the young artist was asked about his drawing, he explained that he had started by taking a photograph of himself sitting by a window at home. He then drew his face from the photograph and replaced the buildings which were outside the window with trees. This gave the picture a softer, more artistic background.

4. Humans need to use energy in order to exist. So it is unsurprising that the way people have been producing energy is largely responsible for current environmental problems. Pollution comes in many forms, but those that are most concerning, because of their impact on health, result from the combustion of fuels in power stations and cars.

5. Clearly, times are changing and while many people are saving for their retirement, many more still need to do so. Most countries have a range of pension schemes that are designed to provide individuals with an income once they stop working. People need to take advantage of these if they are to have sufficient money throughout their retirement years.

6. According to recent research, sunshine and warm weather have a positive effect on our moods. The British Journal of Psychology has published a report in which it claims that anxiety levels fall when temperatures rise, while increased exposure to sunshine makes us think more positively about our lives.

Repeat sentence

About the task type

This is a short-answer speaking task type that tests listening and speaking skills. You have to repeat a sentence that you hear, with correct pronunciation. You will do 10–12 *Repeat sentence* tasks.

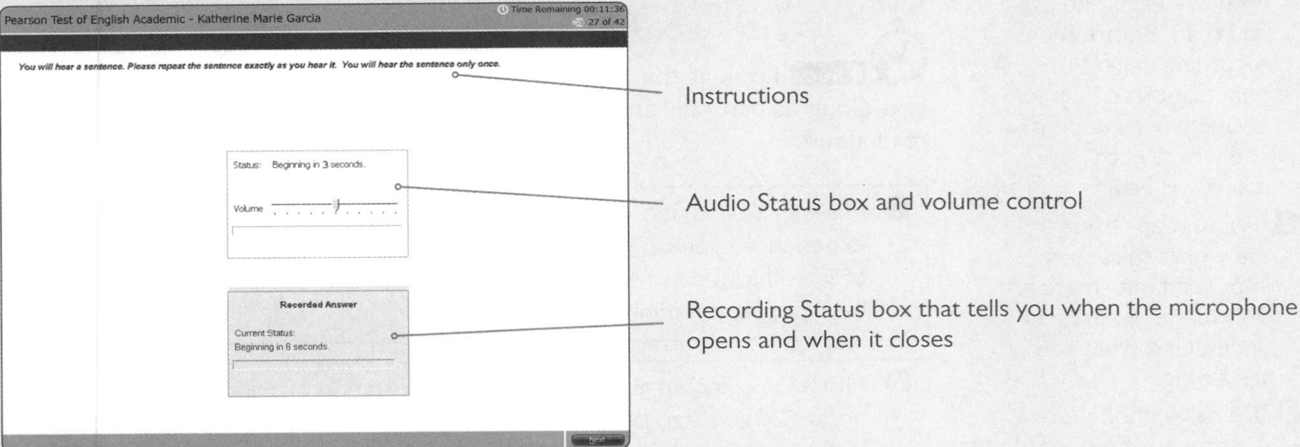

Strategies

Be ready

- The Audio Status box will count down from 3 seconds and then the recording will play.
- Be ready to hear, understand and repeat the short sentence (3 to 9 seconds). Stay focused.

Focus on the meaning

- Listen to the way the speaker groups words into meaningful phrases, and copy this phrasing.
- Listen for the speaker's intonation and try to copy it.
- Listen for the grammatical structure to help you to reconstruct what you have heard.
- There isn't time to write the words.

Speak clearly

- Wait until the blue bar that shows the microphone is open, then speak; there is no tone. Remember, the microphone will close after 3 seconds of silence.
- Take a breath before you speak; this will help you speak clearly.
- Say every word you hear, but if you don't know a word, say what you think you heard.
- Pronounce the vowels and consonants clearly, and link words together as the speaker did.
- Speak at a normal speed and volume, and don't rush – you have plenty of time.
- Don't try to copy the speaker's accent; just speak normally.
- Click 'Next' to move on.

Testing focus Scoring ➤ page 147

Subskills tested

Listening: understanding academic vocabulary; inferring the meaning of unfamiliar words; comprehending variations in tone, speed and accent.

Speaking: speaking for a purpose (to repeat, to inform, to explain); speaking at a natural rate; producing fluent speech; using correct intonation; using correct pronunciation; using correct stress; speaking under timed conditions.

Preparation

- Train your short-term memory by repeating short announcements or advertisements that you hear; ask a friend to read aloud 10–12 short sentences from a magazine for you to repeat each one.
- Develop your understanding of English grammar so that you recognize verb phrases and clause structure. When you hear someone speaking, repeat the words to yourself and think of the structures they used.
- Your score will be higher if you say the correct words in the right sequence, so practise saying phrases with correct word order.
- Use a dictionary where you can listen to the words pronounced in different accents so that when you learn a new word you also know what it sounds like.
- Practise saying new words with the correct syllable stress. Check the dictionary if you are not sure.
- Notice where people put the stress in sentences – the important words are stressed and the other words are weak or unstressed. Try to do this when you speak; your score will be higher if your rhythm, phrasing and stress are smooth and effective.
- Listen to someone giving a talk in a podcast and stop the recording regularly so you can repeat the words you heard. Begin by stopping after 3 or 4 words, then gradually expand until you stop about every 7–9 seconds.
- Listen to podcasts by speakers with different English accents to become familiar with them.

TIP STRIP

1. Listen to the way the speaker groups the words into meaningful phrases, e.g. *such as cost and function, the design of a bridge*.
2. Speak as clearly as you can. If you mumble, your words may not be recognized.
3. Listen to the speaker's intonation and aim to copy this.
4. Listen to the syllable stress on long words, such as *financial* and *available* and say the words the same way.
5. Note how the speaker uses word stress to highlight the important information, for example, *Extra seminars*. Try to do the same.
6. Your score will be improved if you produce correct word sequences including phrasal verbs such as *switch off* and noun phrases such as *electronic devices*.
7. Many words in a sentence are unstressed or 'weak forms', for example in the phrase *as a team, as a* is unstressed. You will not hear weak forms clearly but the grammar tells you they are present.
8. Remember there is no tone before the microphone opens in this task, so start to speak as soon as the Status box changes to 'Recording'.
9. Be prepared for long noun phrases before the verb in some tasks, as in *Detailed analysis of population growth*.
10. You will hear a range of accents in this task, but don't try to copy the accent. Just speak naturally.

Repeat sentence

In the test, there are 10–12 tasks. For each task, you listen and repeat the sentence you hear into the microphone. The wording in the instructions below is the same as you will see in the actual test. See page 14 for help.

▶ 2–11 15 sec. You will hear a sentence. Please repeat the sentence exactly as you hear it. You will hear the sentence only once.

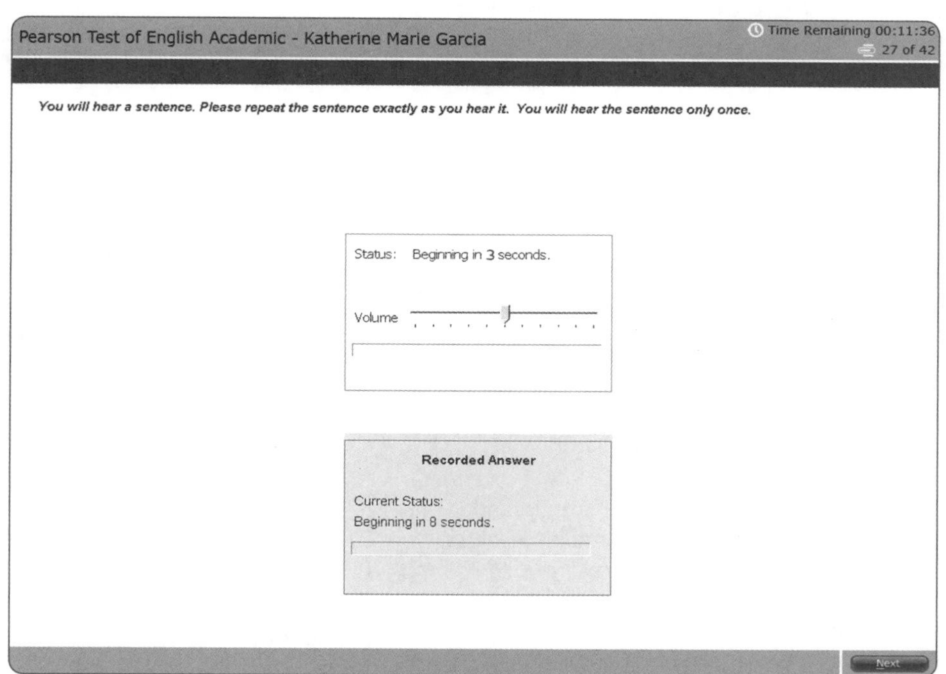

Repeat sentence: Each question is displayed on a new screen.

Describe image

About the task type

This is a long-answer speaking task type that tests speaking skills. You have 40 seconds to describe the information in a graph, chart, map, picture or table. You will do 6–7 *Describe image* tasks.

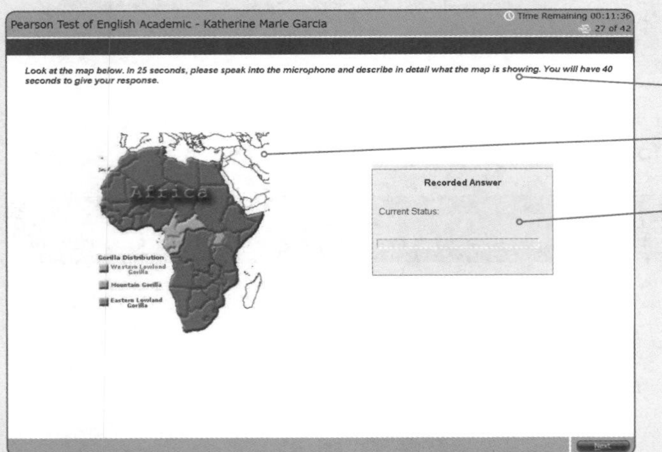

Strategies

Look carefully at the image

- You have 25 seconds before the microphone opens to look carefully at the image.
- Identify the main features or trends, and the names of features or variables in labels. Identify the significant features, major contrasts or changes over time. Think of any implications of the information, or any conclusions that can be drawn.
- Make notes of the main points on your Erasable Noteboard Booklet, and decide the order in which you will describe the information.

Focus on the main points

- After the tone, start with a general statement of what the image is about. Then describe the most important features or trends or contrasts.
- Don't try to describe every detail; use relevant data to illustrate the main points of the information.
- Use your notes to make sure your description is clearly organized.
- Conclude with a comment on any implications or conclusions.

Keep speaking

- Keep speaking. The more you say, the more thorough your description will be.
- If you make an error in the information, don't worry; correct yourself and move on. When the microphone closes, click 'Next'.

Testing focus Scoring ➤ page 148

Subskills tested

Speaking: speaking for a purpose (to repeat, to inform, to explain); supporting an opinion with details, examples and explanations; organizing an oral presentation in a logical way; developing complex ideas within a spoken discourse; using words and phrases appropriate to the context; using correct grammar; speaking at a natural rate; producing fluent speech; using correct intonation; using correct pronunciation; using correct stress; speaking under timed conditions.

Preparation

- Practise interpreting different types of image, including line, bar and pie graphs, process diagrams and maps, that you see in news stories.
- Find an image that interests you. Take brief notes of the main points using key words, with arrows to indicate the order of what you will say. Practise using your notes to organize your description.
- Practise giving an overview by summarizing the information in an image in one sentence. Set a timer so that you are ready to give the overview after 25 seconds.
- You will score higher if you include, as well as all the main points, any developments or implications, or any conclusions that can be drawn.
- Set a timer for 40 seconds and practise describing a picture or graph so you are familiar with the time you have to speak in this task. Then find 6 or 7 images to describe, and practise describing all of them, with 25 seconds to look at each image and 40 seconds to describe it.
- Record yourself describing an image then compare your response with the image to check how complete your description was.
- Practise using words and phrases used to describe amounts (*more than, less than, approximately*) and trends (*rose, fell, fluctuated, remained stable*), as well as comparatives and superlatives (*greatest, highest, lowest, higher than, lower than*).

Describe image

TIP STRIP

1. Look at the image carefully and make sure you understand what it shows. If you have a graph, look closely at both axes. In this graph, the vertical axis shows the percentage of the world population NOT the population figures.
2. If there are two graphs or charts, this means you have to make comparisons. Look for the most significant similarities and differences.

In the test, there are 6–7 tasks. For each task, you look at the image and describe it into the microphone. The wording in the instructions below is the same as you will see in the actual test. See page 16 for help.

1 **40 sec.** Look at the graph below. In 25 seconds, please speak into the microphone and describe in detail what the graph is showing. You will have 40 seconds to give your response.

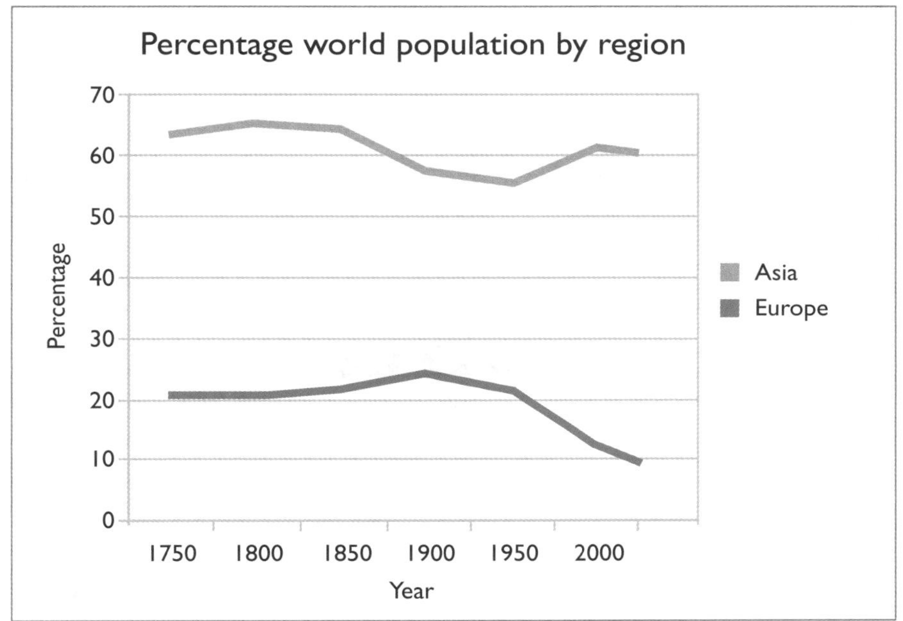

2 **40 sec.** Look at the charts below. In 25 seconds, please speak into the microphone and describe in detail what the charts are showing. You will have 40 seconds to give your response.

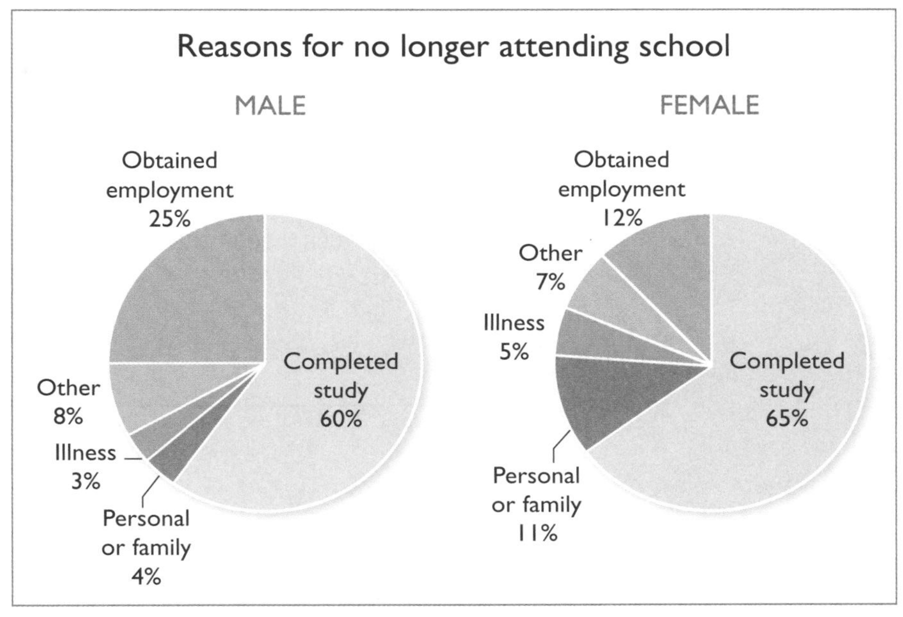

TEST 1

SPEAKING

TEST 1

SPEAKING

TIP STRIP

3 Look at the overall idea or pattern and make sure you describe that. Don't just focus on the details. You will score higher if you include possible developments, conclusions or implications.

4 When a graph gives information on large numbers or quantities, make sure you say these correctly. In this case, the graph title tells you that it shows figures in millions of dollars, not hundreds.

3 40 sec. Look at the chart below. In 25 seconds, please speak into the microphone and describe in detail what the chart is showing. You will have 40 seconds to give your response.

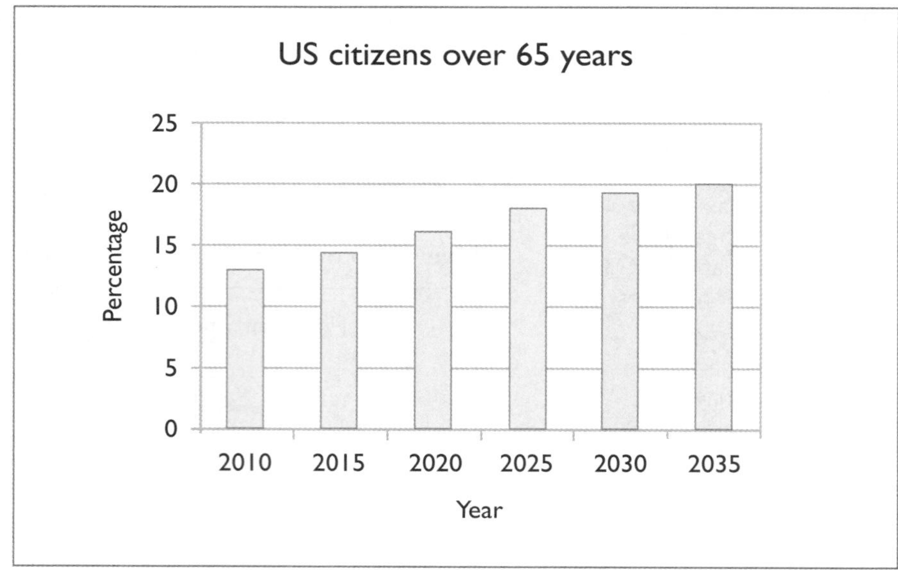

4 40 sec. Look at the graph below. In 25 seconds, please speak into the microphone and describe in detail what the graph is showing. You will have 40 seconds to give your response.

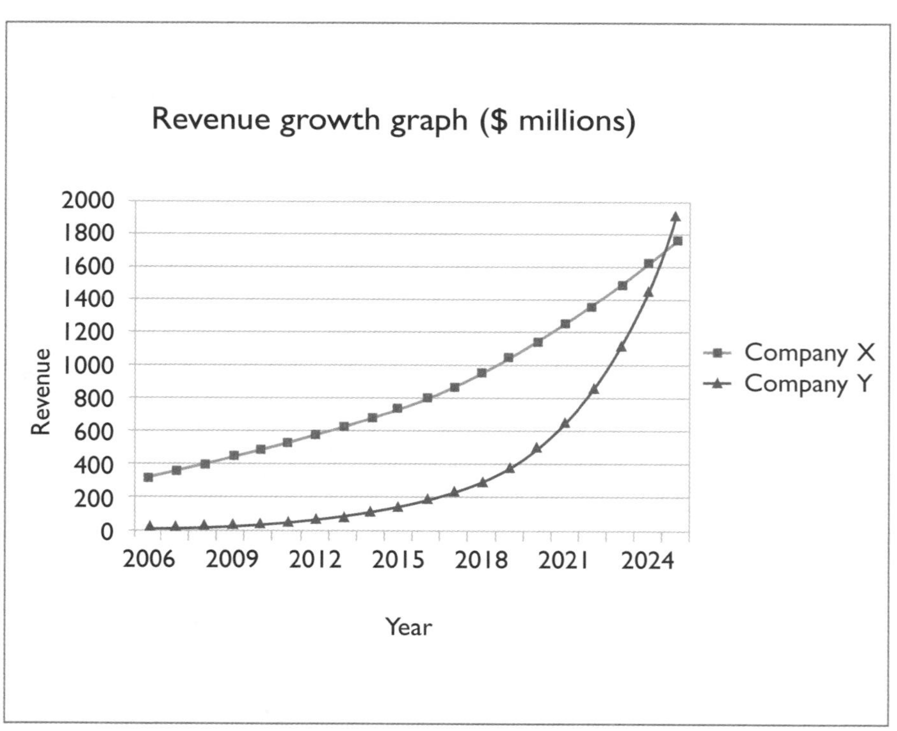

TIP STRIP

5 You cannot always describe every point on a graph. Look at the trend. If it is quite steady, describe what it shows overall and only highlight significant differences.

6 If you have a diagram of a process, start by describing the different parts or elements of the process and then move on to describing the process itself.

5 40 sec. Look at the graph below. In 25 seconds, please speak into the microphone and describe in detail what the graph is showing. You will have 40 seconds to give your response.

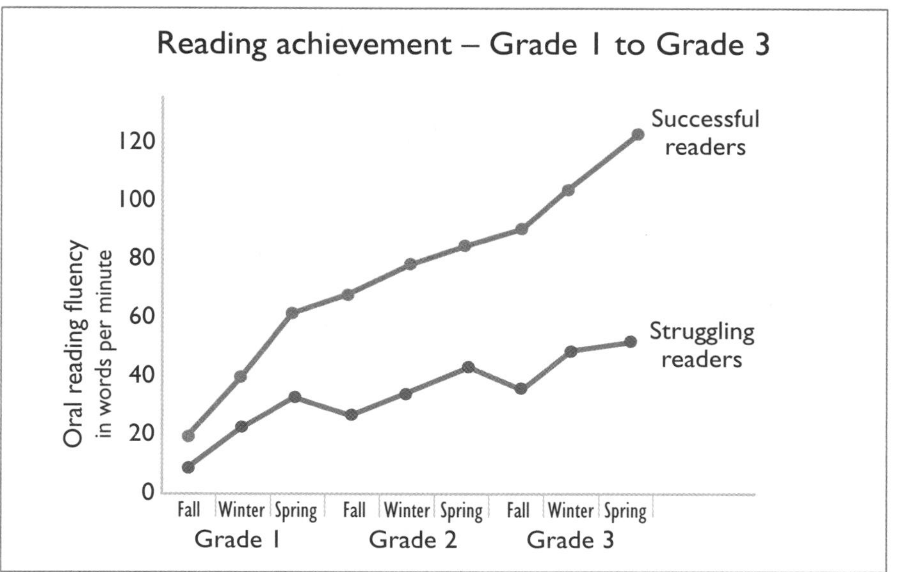

6 40 sec. Look at the diagram below. In 25 seconds, please speak into the microphone and describe in detail what the diagram is showing. You will have 40 seconds to give your response.

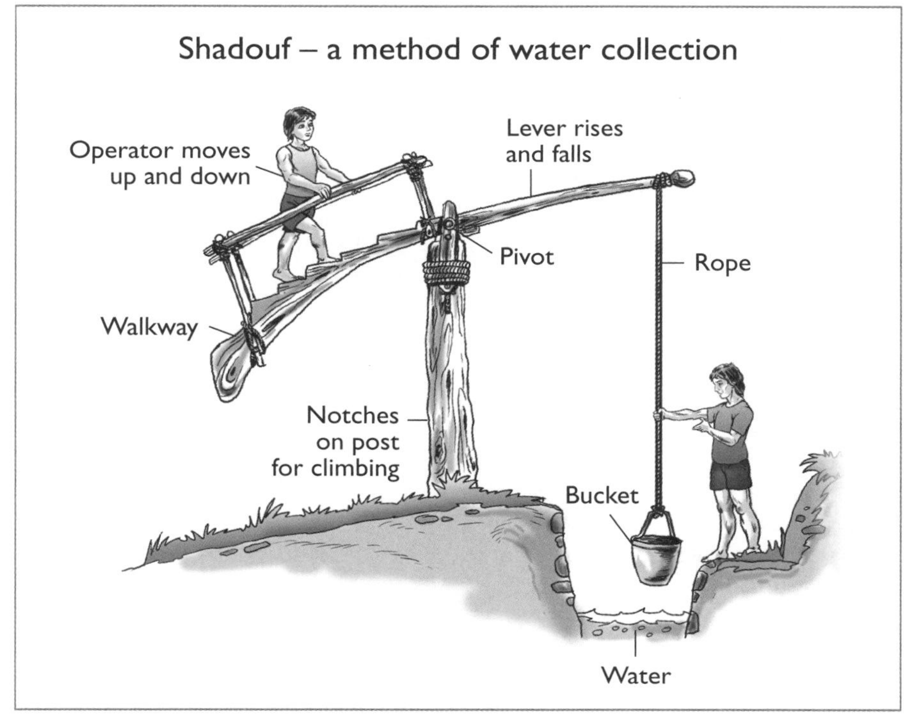

TEST 1 SPEAKING

Re-tell lecture

About the task type

This is a long-answer speaking task type that tests both listening and speaking skills. You have to re-tell in your own words the information in a 60–90 second lecture. You will do 3–4 *Re-tell lecture* tasks.

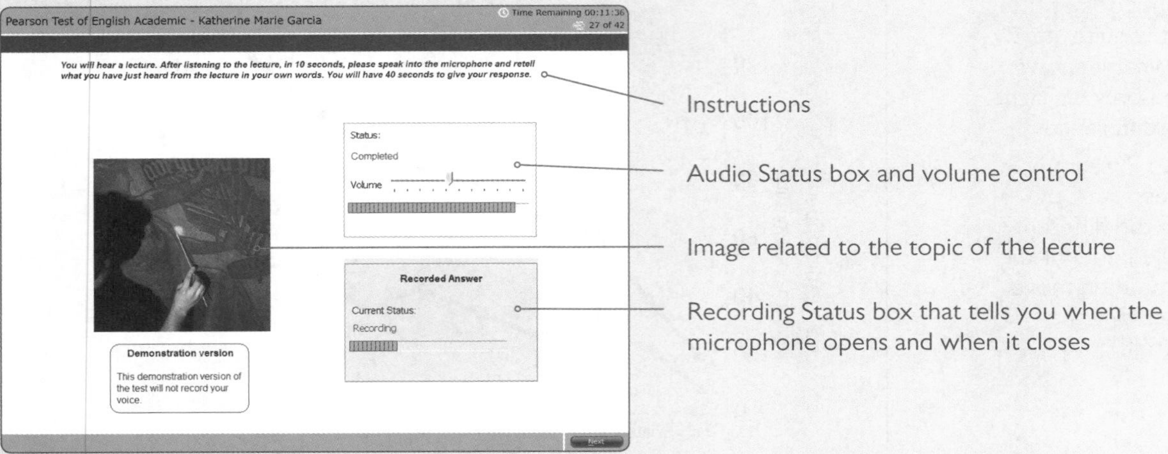

Pearson Test of English Academic - Katherine Marie Garcia
Time Remaining 00:11:36
27 of 42
You will hear a lecture. After listening to the lecture, in 10 seconds, please speak into the microphone and retell what you have just heard from the lecture in your own words. You will have 40 seconds to give your response.
Status:
Completed
Volume
Recorded Answer
Current Status:
Recording
Demonstration version
This demonstration version of the test will not record your voice.
Next
Instructions
Audio Status box and volume control
Image related to the topic of the lecture
Recording Status box that tells you when the microphone opens and when it closes

STRATEGIES

Strategies

Be ready

- Before the recording begins, look at the image to help you to anticipate the topic of the lecture.
- Be ready to take notes on the Erasable Noteboard Booklet.
- Remember you can change the volume using the slider in the Audio Status box.

Take notes as you listen

- As you listen, take notes of the main and supporting ideas.
- Don't try to write down everything you hear. Use key words, abbreviations, symbols and arrows to capture the most important ideas and organize them so you can use your notes to speak.
- When the recording stops, you have 10 seconds before a tone indicates that the microphone is open and the blue bar appears in the Recording Status box. Use this time to plan how you will begin, and the order in which you will present the information.

Summarize

- Use your notes to summarize all the main points and add as many supporting details or examples as you can, as well as any implications or conclusions.
- Speak clearly and at a natural pace. You have 40 seconds to re-tell the information so you do not need to rush. When the microphone closes, click 'Next'.

Testing focus Scoring ➤ page 148

Subskills tested

Listening: identifying the topic, theme or main ideas; identifying supporting points or examples; identifying a speaker's purpose, style, tone or attitude; understanding academic vocabulary; inferring the meaning of unfamiliar words; comprehending explicit and implicit information; comprehending concrete and abstract information; classifying and categorizing information; following an oral sequencing of information; comprehending variations in tone, speed and accent.

Speaking: speaking for a purpose (to repeat, to inform, to explain); supporting an opinion with details, examples and explanations; organizing an oral presentation in a logical way; developing complex ideas within a spoken discourse; using words and phrases appropriate to the context; using correct grammar; speaking at a natural rate; producing fluent speech; using correct intonation; using correct pronunciation; using correct stress; speaking under timed conditions.

Preparation

- Develop your own techniques for rapid note-taking. Decide on your own abbreviations and symbols and practise using them so they become automatic.
- Practise starting your response with a topic sentence that introduces the topic and main idea.
- The best responses will include any conclusions or implications, so always consider the significance of the information.
- Listen to 30 seconds of a lecture, noting the key words, then stop the audio and state the main point. Repeat this, extending the time to 90 seconds.
- Find podcasts of lectures with a transcript. Highlight the signal words that indicate the main points and the examples, or evidence, or opposing arguments, then listen for them in the audio. Use the signal words in your own re-telling of the lecture.
- Find 3 or 4 podcasts of lectures and listen to the first 90 seconds, taking notes. Time yourself for 40 seconds re-telling the extract from the lecture using your notes, then move on to the next one.

Re-tell lecture

In the test, there are 3–4 tasks. For each task, you see an image on the screen. Listen to the lecture and then speak into the microphone. The wording in the instructions below is the same as you will see in the actual test. See page 20 for help.

You will hear a lecture. After listening to the lecture, in 10 seconds, please speak into the microphone and retell what you have just heard from the lecture in your own words. You will have 40 seconds to give your response.

1 ▶ 12

2 ▶ 13

3 ▶ 14

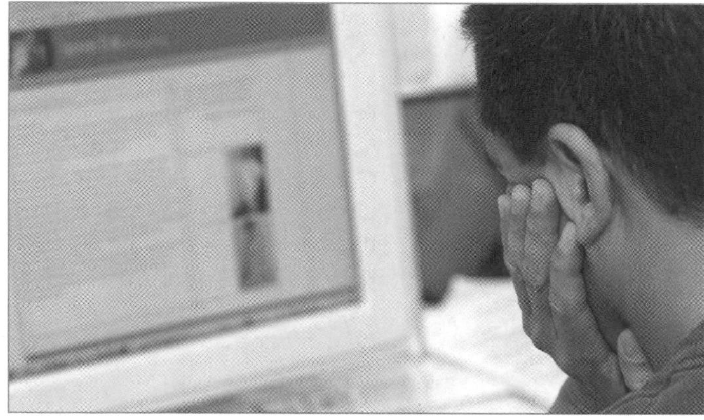

TIP STRIP

1. Use the image to anticipate the vocabulary you might hear. For example, the picture of a polluted city means you are likely to hear *air pollution*, *industrial pollution*, *smog*, *source of pollution*, *health problems*, *motor vehicles*, and so on.
2. Be ready to take notes. Don't try to write every word. Use key words, symbols and arrows to note the main and supporting ideas. Stay focused and keep taking notes until the lecture stops. You will improve your score if you include relevant detail with the main points.
3. Listen and take note of any signposts to help you recognize the main points. Phrases such as *There are three main areas* can guide your note taking. If your notes follow the speaker's sequencing, you can use this to organize your own response. Remember, after the audio stops you only have ten seconds before the tone sounds to tell you to begin speaking, so well-organized notes are important.

Answer short question

About the task type

This is a short-answer speaking task type that tests listening and speaking skills. You have to respond to a short question, in one or a few words. You will do 10–12 *Answer short question* tasks.

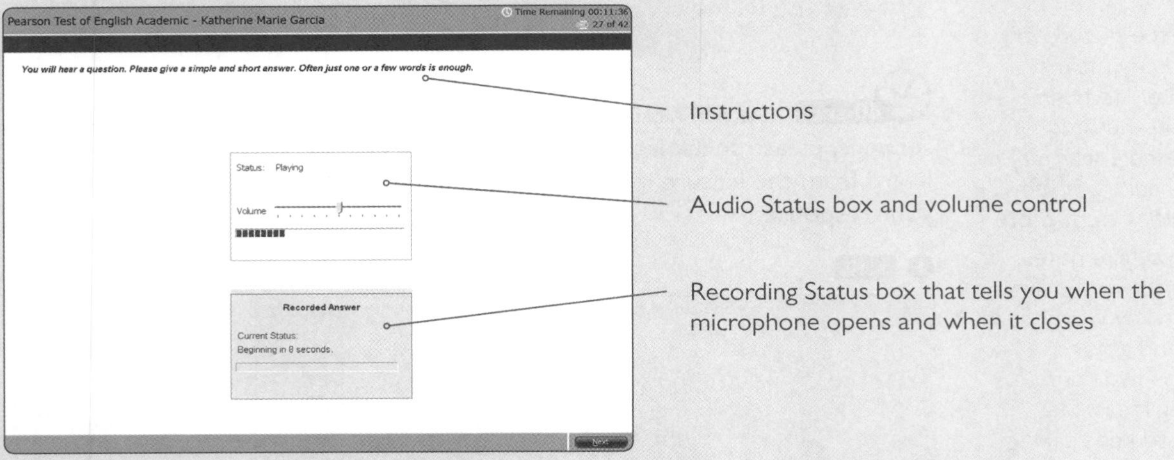

STRATEGIES

Strategies

Stay focused

- In the 3 seconds before the audio begins for each task, focus on the task so you are ready to understand the question.
- The questions are short, and you must answer as soon as the microphone opens, so keep your concentration through all the tasks.
- Don't let your mind wander as there is no time to 'tune in' to what you will hear.

Understand the question

- Listen for the question word (*who, what, when, how, why*) that will help you to understand the question.
- Do not be afraid that you will not have the specific knowledge needed; all the questions are about topics that every educated person knows.
- There is one correct answer that is usually one word or a short phrase.

Speak clearly

- Speak when the blue recording bar appears in the Recording Status box (there is no tone). The microphone will close if there is silence for more than 3 seconds.
- If you realize you have made a mistake, correct yourself, as the score depends on the correct word or words only. Once you have answered, click 'Next'.

Testing focus Scoring ➤ page 149

Subskills tested

Listening: identifying the topic, theme or main ideas; understanding academic vocabulary; inferring the meaning of unfamiliar words.

Speaking: speaking for a purpose (to repeat, to inform, to explain); using words and phrases appropriate to the context; speaking under timed conditions.

Preparation

- To practise giving quick responses to short questions, work with a friend to write a set of short questions on cards on general knowledge topics you know well, then exchange cards and ask each other the questions (*What satellite of the earth lights the sky at night? Where would you find whales? What part of their body do birds use to fly?* etc.). Answer with one or a few words only.
- Expand your vocabulary by developing association balloons: take a common word, put it inside a circle, then add any words you associate with that word. Use a dictionary and a thesaurus to add to the words in your circle, for example, for *medicine*, you might put *hospital, doctor, nurse, disease, illness, x-ray, health, exercise, bones, veins, surgery*.
- Practise understanding question forms by writing a series of short statements about a topic you know well, then converting them all to questions. Ask a friend to ask you the questions in random order, and you answer them.
- Practise using question forms across as many tenses as you can, e.g. *What does …, What did …, What will …, What would …* .
- Check the pronunciation of any new words you learn by using a dictionary with the words recorded. Make sure you know where the stress falls within the word.
- Practise listening for the stressed words in questions you hear. Repeat the question to yourself and clap on the stressed words. Remember that the stressed words carry the main meaning in a question.

Answer short question

In the test, there are 10–12 tasks. For each task, you hear a question and speak your answer into the microphone. The wording in the instructions below is the same as you will see in the actual test. See page 22 for help.

▸ 15-24  10 sec. You will hear a question. Please give a simple and short answer. Often just one or a few words is enough.

TIP STRIP

1. Start your answer as soon as the Recording Status box changes to 'Recording'. If you wait longer than three seconds, you will lose your opportunity to answer and the recording will move on to the next question.
2. This task type is not individually timed. You must click 'Next' to move to the next task after you have given your response. The timer for the Speaking section will continue running, so once the microphone closes, click 'Next' and move on.
3. Follow the instructions and only give a short answer. For example, if the answer is *stage*, then *stage*, *a stage*, *the stage*, *it's called a stage*, *It's a stage* will all be correct and will score the same marks. The important word is *stage*.
4. Sometimes you can use words in the question to help you answer, e.g. the word *desk* is often used with the answer to form a well-known phrase.
5. The answer will usually not include words in the question. For example, *designer* or *building designer* is not the correct answer for this question because it's too general; it's not the specific job title.
6. Listen carefully to the whole question. For this question, you might pay a cheque or cash to a landlord; but these are ways of paying for something, not the term used for the amount of money you pay.
7. Listen for the question word, e.g. *who*, *what*, *how*. In this question, *What do we call* tells you the answer is the name of something, and *meal* tells you the 'something' is to do with food.
8. Remember that you will do 10–12 tasks of this type. Keep your concentration as you move through the questions.
9. Once the microphone closes, you cannot change your answer. If you realize your first answer was not correct, keep speaking and give the correct answer. You have ten seconds to give your response, but the microphone will close if there are more than three seconds of silence.
10. Don't pause in the middle of your answer for more than three seconds. If you do so, the recording will move on to the next question and your answer will be incomplete.

Summarize written text

About the task type

This is a short-answer writing task type that tests reading and writing skills. You have 10 minutes to write a one-sentence summary of a reading passage. You will do 2–3 *Summarize written text* tasks.

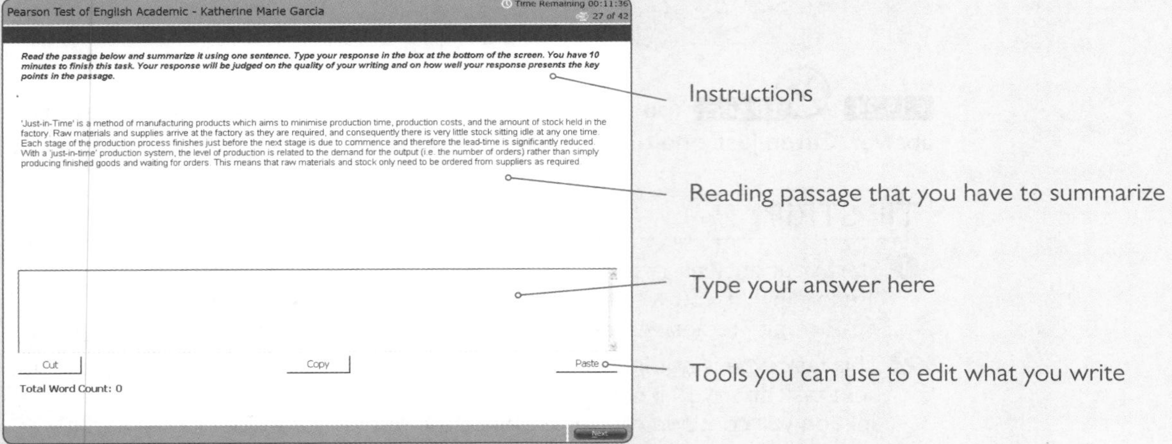

STRATEGIES

Strategies

Use your reading skills

- Take the time to read the passage calmly. First, skim for the general topic, then read carefully for the main ideas.
- Note the main idea and supporting ideas using key words, and arrows and symbols to indicate how the ideas are organized. Effective note-taking will ensure that your summary has all the main points.

Construct your summary

- Type the main point of the passage in the box, then add the supporting or other details.
- Remember, your response must be one sentence only, between 5 and 75 words, so you must use grammatical structures and punctuation that allow you to include all your points within one sentence.
- Use the 'Cut', 'Copy', and 'Paste' buttons to move text around. There is a word counter below the writing box, and a timer running at the top of the screen.

Check your writing

- Take a few minutes to check your grammar and vocabulary. Does your sentence begin with a capital letter and end with a full stop?
- Your response will not be scored if it is more than one sentence, or if it is written all in capital letters.
- At the end of 10 minutes, the screen will stop responding.

Testing focus Scoring ➤ page 149

Subskills tested

Reading: reading a passage under timed conditions; identifying a writer's purpose, style, tone or attitude; comprehending explicit and implicit information; comprehending concrete and abstract information.

Writing: writing a summary; writing under timed conditions; taking notes while reading a text; synthesizing information; writing to meet strict length requirements; communicating the main points of a reading passage in writing; using words and phrases appropriate to the context; using correct grammar and spelling.

Preparation

- Practise skimming short texts quickly (up to 300 words) to identify the main points. In a longer article, stop reading after each paragraph and summarize the main point in one sentence.
- Work with a friend to agree on what are the main ideas and supporting ideas in texts.
- Develop your own techniques for rapid note-taking. Decide on your own abbreviations and symbols and practise using them so they become automatic.
- Revise complex structures such as subordinate clauses and the use of conjunctions that will allow you to include more ideas within one sentence. Analyze long sentences in texts to identify how the writer has constructed each one.
- Find a short text (up to 300 words) and time yourself reading and summarizing it. Take one minute to skim for the main idea, then 2 minutes to read carefully and take notes. Spend 5 minutes writing a one sentence summary, and 2 minutes checking your work.
- Compare your summary to the original text. The best response will clearly summarize the main idea and condense essential supporting ideas.
- Find a set of 2 or 3 short texts and time yourself summarizing them, one after the other. Make sure you only spend 10 minutes on each text.

Summarize written text

TIP STRIP

In order to get the main points into one sentence, you will need to use grammatical features, such as conjunctions (*and, but,* etc.), conditional clauses (*if, when,* etc.) and relative clauses (*who, which, that,* etc.).

In the test, there are 2–3 tasks. Each task has a text on the screen. You type your summary of the text into the box at the bottom of the screen. The wording in the instructions below is the same as you will see in the actual test. See page 24 for help.

1 **10 min.** **Read the passage below and summarize it using one sentence. Type your response in the box at the bottom of the screen. You have 10 minutes to finish this task. Your response will be judged on the quality of your writing and on how well your response presents the key points in the passage.**

By far the most popular and most consumed drink in the world is water, but it may come as no surprise that the second most popular beverage is tea. Although tea was originally grown only in certain parts of Asia – in countries such as China, Burma and India – it is now a key export product in more than 50 countries around the globe. Countries that grow tea, however, need to have the right tropical climate, which includes up to 200 centimetres of rainfall per year to encourage fast growth, and temperatures that range from ten to 35 degrees centigrade. They also need to have quite specific geographical features, such as high altitudes to promote the flavour and taste of the tea, and land that can offer plenty of shade in the form of other trees and vegetation to keep the plants cool and fresh. Together these conditions contribute to the production of the wide range of high-quality teas that are in such huge demand among the world's consumers. There is green tea, jasmine tea, earl grey tea, peppermint tea, tea to help you sleep, tea to promote healing and tea to relieve stress; but above all, tea is a social drink that seems to suit the palates and consumption habits of human beings in general.

....

....

....

....

....

2 10 min. **Read the passage below and summarize it using one sentence. Type your response in the box at the bottom of the screen. You have 10 minutes to finish this task. Your response will be judged on the quality of your writing and on how well your response presents the key points in the passage.**

TIP STRIP

Remember to only write one sentence. Make sure your answer has a capital letter at the start and ends with a full stop. Also, check that you have used commas appropriately within your sentence.

With all the discussions about protecting the earth and saving the planet, it is easy to forget that we also need to preserve the many species of fish that live in the oceans. In developed countries, much larger quantities of fish are consumed than was the case a century ago when fish only featured on the menu once a week. These days, fish has become a popular healthy alternative to meat and this has created a demand for species such as cod, mackerel and tuna that far outstrips the demands of the previous generation. Throughout the world too, increasing consumption during the past 30 years has meant that the shallow parts of the ocean have been overfished in an effort to supply homes, shops and restaurants with the quantities of fish that they require. Yet despite the sophisticated fishing techniques of today, catches are smaller than they were a century or more ago. What is more, boats are having to drop their nets much deeper into the oceans and the fish they are coming up with are smaller and weigh less than they used to. While government controls have had some effect on fish stocks, the future does not offer a promising picture. Experts predict large-scale extinctions and an irreversibly damaging effect on entire ecosystems, unless greater efforts are made to conserve fish stocks and prevent overfishing in the world's waters.

Write essay

About the task type

This is a long-answer writing task type that tests writing skills. You have 20 minutes to write a 200–300 word persuasive or argumentative essay on a given topic. You will do 1–2 *Write essay* tasks.

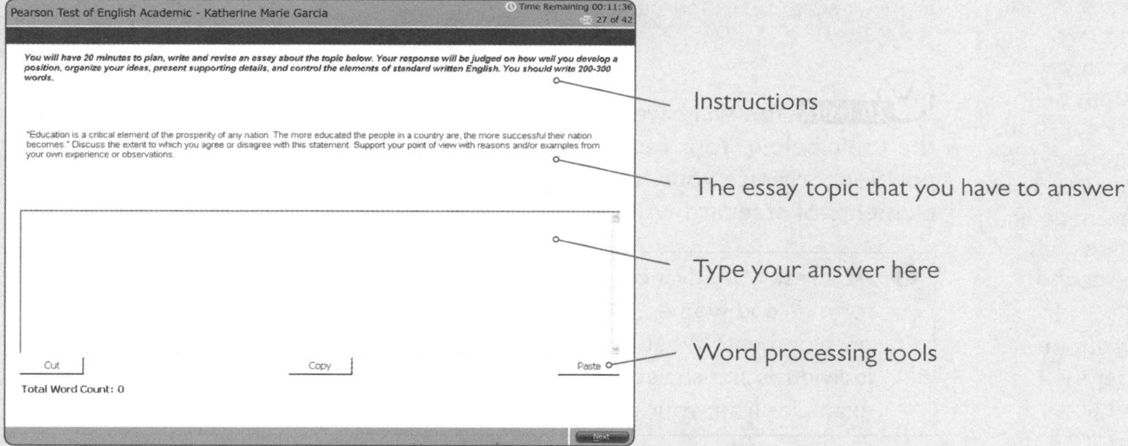

Strategies

Analyze and plan

- First, analyze the essay task. Identify the key words that tell you the general topic, then look for the particular aspect of the topic you are being asked about (often in the form of a statement of a position).
- Look closely at the task to see exactly what you have to do – agree/disagree, answer specific questions, etc.
- Use your Erasable Noteboard Booklet to plan your essay. Note the ideas you want to include, and decide how you will order them.

Write your essay

- Use your outline notes to present your position on the task, and support your opinion with evidence and examples. Remember that it doesn't matter what your opinion is as long as you argue it clearly and with support.
- Make sure you cover all the required aspects of the question.
- Make sure your essay is well organized, with a new paragraph for each new idea, to develop your argument.

Check your writing

- Save a few minutes to check your writing. You will lose marks for poor grammar and for spelling mistakes.
- After 20 minutes the screen will stop responding, so click 'Next' and move on.

Testing focus Scoring ➤ page 150

Subskills tested

Writing: writing for a purpose (to learn, to inform, to persuade); supporting an opinion with details, examples and explanations; organizing sentences and paragraphs in a logical way; developing complex ideas within a complete essay; using words and phrases appropriate to the context; using correct grammar; using correct spelling; using correct mechanics; writing under timed conditions.

Preparation

- Look at the *Write essay* tasks in this book and in *The Official Guide to PTE Academic*. Circle the topic in each one, then underline the particular aspect of the topic you must write about. Identify the instruction that tells you exactly what you must do – agree/disagree, answer specific questions, etc.
- Practise developing outlines for essay topics. Look again at the essay topics in this book and in *The Official Guide to PTE Academic*, and prepare quick outlines for each one. Remember that a response that does not address the topic will be scored zero.
- Practise writing introductory paragraphs, with one sentence that makes a general statement on the topic and a second sentence that introduces your opinion.
- Practise writing conclusions that re-state or summarize your argument in one sentence.
- Make a list of signpost words you can use to show how an argument is organized, such as *Firstly, Secondly, However, In addition, On the other hand*, etc. Write paragraphs that use these signpost words.
- Write 250 words on one essay topic on your computer and time how long it takes you to do this. Decide how much time you can spend planning your essay, how much time writing, and how much time checking.
- Practise writing without using the spell-checker and grammar checker on your computer so that you learn to recognize wrong spellings. You cannot use a spell-checker or grammar checker in the actual test.

Write essay

> **TIP STRIP**
>
> ❶ In this type of essay, you need to write about the questions you are asked. In Topic 1, there are two questions, so you must answer both of them. Read the questions carefully. Make sure you know what any pronouns refer to. For example, in Topic 1 what does *this* refer to in the second sentence?
>
> ❷ Think carefully about the question before you start. Sometimes it helps to re-word a statement as a question, e.g. for Topic 2: *Should schools prepare students for university, rather than work?*

In the test, there are 1–2 tasks. For each task, the essay question is on the screen. You type your essay into the box on the screen. The wording in the instructions below is the same as you will see in the actual test. See page 27 for help.

20 min. You will have 20 minutes to plan, write and revise an essay about the topic below. Your response will be judged on how well you develop a position, organize your ideas, present supporting details, and control the elements of standard written English. You should write 200–300 words.

❶ As a result of advances in medical care, average life expectancy is increasing for men and women. Do you think most people will see this as a positive development? What are the disadvantages of an ageing population for individuals and society? Support your point of view with reasons and/or examples from your own experience or observations.

❷ 'Schools should prepare students for university, rather than for work.' How far do you agree with this statement? Support your point of view with reasons and/or examples from your own experience or observations.

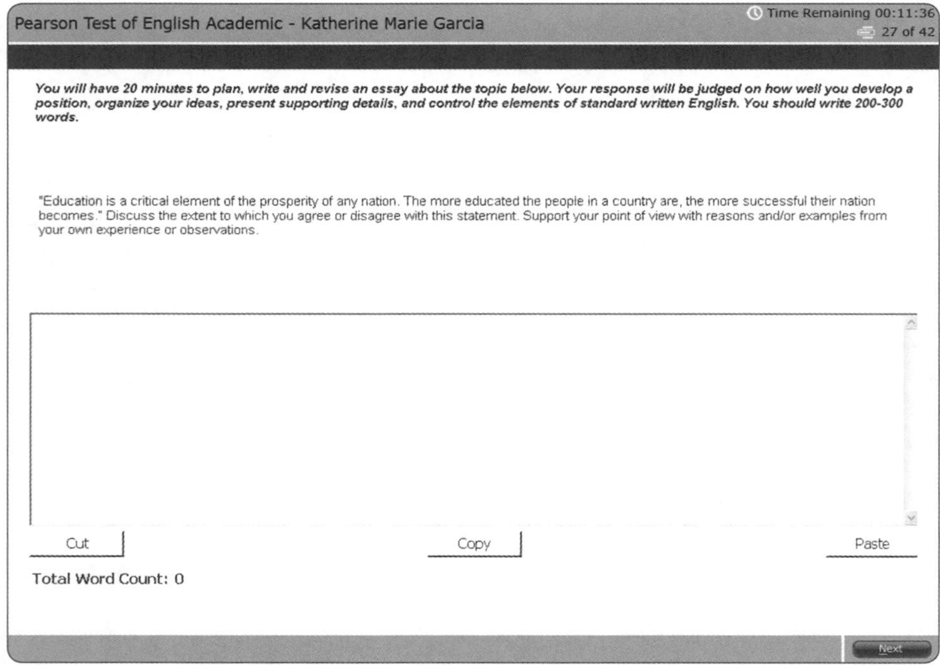

Write essay: Each question is displayed on a new screen.

Overview: Reading

Part 2 of the PTE Academic test is Reading. This part tests your ability to understand written English in an academic environment.

The table shows what you will see in the test, which you will take on a computer. When practising with this book, you will have to write your written answers in the book, your notebook or on your own computer.

Part 2: Reading				
Reading (total time 32–41 minutes)				
Task type	Number of tasks	Task description	Skills assessed	Text/ Recording length
Multiple-choice, choose single answer	2–3	After reading a text, answer a multiple-choice question on the content or tone of the text by selecting one response.	reading	text up to 300 words
Multiple-choice, choose multiple answers	2–3	After reading a text, answer a multiple-choice question on the content or tone of the text by selecting more than one response.	reading	text up to 300 words
Re-order paragraphs	2–3	Several text boxes appear on screen in random order. Put the text boxes in the correct order.	reading	text up to 150 words
Reading: Fill in the blanks	4–5	A text appears on screen with several blanks. Drag words or phrases from the blue box to fill in the blanks.	reading	text up to 80 words
Reading & writing: Fill in the blanks	5–6	A text appears on screen with several blanks. Fill in the blanks by selecting words from several drop-down lists of response options.	reading and writing	text up to 300 words

You may take notes using the Erasable Noteboard Booklet and pen, and use these notes as a guide when answering the tasks.

Authentic texts about academic subjects in the humanities, natural sciences or social sciences are presented. Although you may not be familiar with the topics presented, all the information you need to answer the tasks is contained in the texts.

Reading task types are not timed individually. You can refer to the timer in the upper right-hand corner of the computer screen, *Time Remaining,* which counts down the time remaining for the Reading part.

Multiple-choice, choose single answer

About the task type

This is a multiple-choice reading task type that tests reading skills. You have to select a single answer to a question about information in a text. You will do 2–3 *Multiple-choice, choose single answer* tasks.

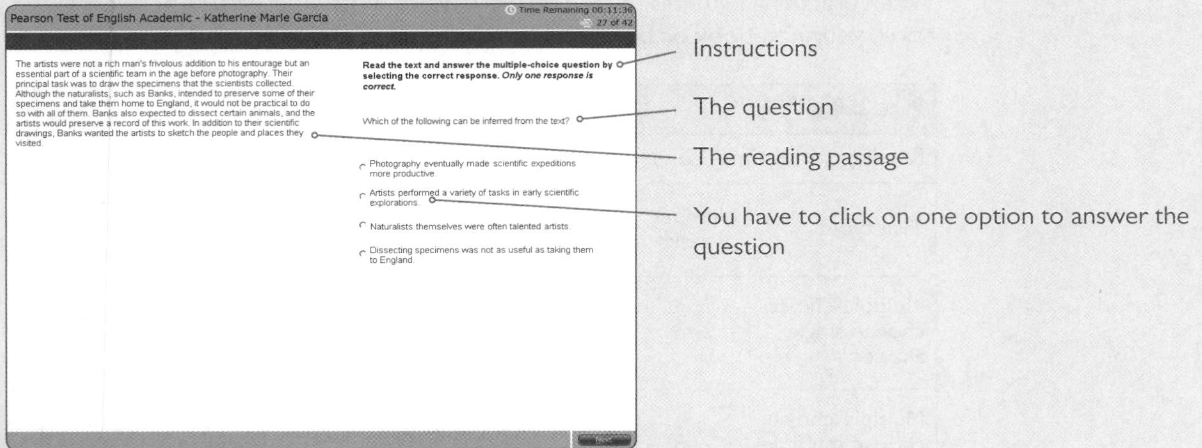

Strategies

Read with purpose

- Read the question before you read the passage. This will tell you what information you are looking for in the text. It could be the main idea, the writer's purpose or attitude, some detailed information, or inferences.
- Next, skim the text to get an idea of the general content and the development of the ideas. Don't worry if you don't understand every word.

Select the option

- From the prompt, identify whether the answer you need is located in the whole text or in part of it, then read carefully the whole text or the relevant part.
- Remember, the options may use synonyms for words in the passage, not the exact words.
- If you don't know an important word in the text, try to guess its meaning from the context.
- Answer the question by clicking on one option or on its radio button ○.

Confirm your choice

- After you have chosen an option, compare each of the other options to the text to eliminate each one. If you change your mind, click on the option again to de-select it, then click on the correct option.
- Be aware of the time and don't spend too much time on one task. Click 'Next' and move on.

Testing focus Scoring ➤ page 152

Subskills tested

Reading: any of the following depending on the task: identifying the topic, theme or main ideas; identifying the relationships between sentences and paragraphs; evaluating the quality and usefulness of texts; identifying a writer's purpose, style, tone or attitude; identifying supporting points or examples; reading for overall organization and connections between pieces of information; reading for information to infer meanings or find relationships; identifying specific details, facts, opinions, definitions or sequences of events; inferring the meaning of unfamiliar words.

Preparation

- Practise skimming short texts of about one paragraph to answer this question: *What is the writer's main point?* Summarize the main point in a short sentence.
- Practise skimming short texts to answer this question: *What is the writer's purpose in this passage?* (to criticize, to argue, to persuade the reader, to describe, to explain, etc.).
- Practise identifying the topic sentences in paragraphs; this helps to identify the main theme.
- Take notes of the information in a text and use arrows to show how the writer's ideas develop.
- Highlight the cohesive devices used in a text, such as pronoun use, article use, substitution, etc.
- Highlight any words you don't know in a text and practise guessing what they mean from the context. Check your guess in a dictionary.
- Work with a friend to see if you agree on what is the main point and what are the supporting points in a text. Identify the signpost words that indicate evidence, support, details, examples, or opposing arguments.
- Expand your vocabulary by creating lists of words with their synonyms. Use a thesaurus to find new words with the same or similar meanings. When you learn a new word, find an example of how it's used in context, for example in a learner's dictionary.

Multiple-choice, choose single answer

TIP STRIP

❶ Read the question before the options and decide what you need to read for. If you are looking for the 'writer's main purpose', you are reading for the overall idea or argument.

❷ If you do not understand a word in the question, check to see whether it has been explained in the passage. In this passage, *innovation* refers back to *any new technology or device*.

In the test, there are 2–3 tasks. For each task, you read the text on the left of the screen and look at the options on the right of the screen. You click the button next to the answer you think is correct. The wording in the instructions below is the same as you will see in the actual test. See page 30 for help.

Read the text and answer the multiple-choice question by selecting the correct response. ***Only one response is correct.***

❶ Huge reserves of energy have been found in rocks far below the surface of the ground in Britain. It is estimated that the north and southwest regions could hold enough energy in the form of heat to provide power for millions of homes. In fact, up to a fifth of Britain's energy could be provided by this geothermal source. Extracting the heat and converting it into electricity is difficult and expensive. Thousands of bore holes would be needed; but once they were in place, the heat would keep regenerating indefinitely.

What is the writer's main purpose in this paragraph?

- ○ A to show how common the use of geothermal power is in Britain
- ○ B to describe the problems related to using geothermal power in Britain
- ○ C to highlight the potential benefits of geothermal power for Britain
- ○ D to give a detailed description of how geothermal energy is produced in Britain

❷ People tend to think that any new technology or device is an act of genius; something that has required vision and insight to create and then develop into a marketable product. The fact is that innovations were often already 'out there' in the public domain in some form or another. They tend to evolve from notions that have been around for years but that had not, until that point, been suitably adapted. One expert calls this the 'long nose' approach to innovation, whereby new concepts come into the world slowly, gradually revealing all they have to offer.

What is the writer's main point about innovation?

- ○ A Many new products fail to interest consumers.
- ○ B New products are not always based on new ideas.
- ○ C Creators of new products require a unique set of skills.
- ○ D New products are easy to distinguish from old ones.

Multiple-choice, choose multiple answers

About the task type

This is a multiple-choice reading task type that tests reading skills. More than one response is correct in answer to a question about a text. You will do 2–3 *Multiple-choice, choose multiple answers* tasks.

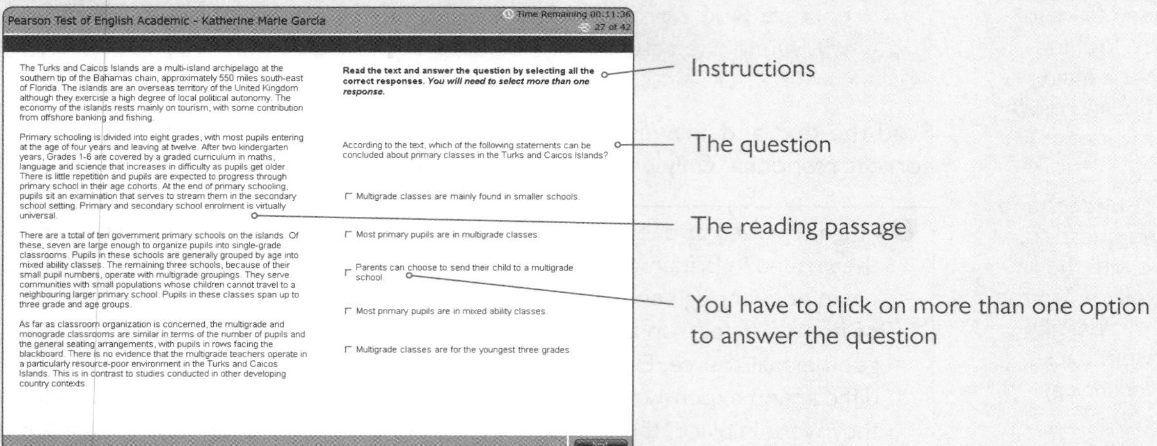

Strategies

Read the question first

- Read the question before you read the passage. This will tell you what information you are looking for in the text. It could be the main ideas, the writer's purpose or attitude, some detailed information, or inferences.
- Next, skim the text to get an idea of the general content and the development of the ideas. Don't worry if you don't understand every word.

Read for a purpose

- From the prompt, identify whether the answers you need are located in the whole text or in parts of it, then read carefully the whole text or the relevant parts.
- Remember, the options may use synonyms for words in the passage, not the exact words.
- If you don't know an important word in the text, try to guess its meaning from the context.
- Answer the question by clicking on more than one option or on their checkboxes.

Confirm your choices

- After you have chosen the options, compare each of the other options to the text to eliminate each one. If you change your mind, click on the option again to de-select it then click on the correct option.
- Be aware of the time and don't spend too much time on one task.

Testing focus Scoring ➤ page 152

Subskills tested

Reading: any of the following depending on the task: identifying the topic, theme or main ideas; identifying the relationships between sentences and paragraphs; evaluating the quality and usefulness of texts; identifying a writer's purpose, style, tone or attitude; identifying supporting points or examples; reading for overall organization and connections between pieces of information; reading for information to infer meanings or find relationships; identifying specific details, facts, opinions, definitions or sequences of events; inferring the meaning of unfamiliar words.

Preparation

- Practise skimming longer texts of several paragraphs to answer this question: *What are the writer's main points?* Summarize the main points.
- Practise skimming longer texts to answer this question: *What were the writer's goals in writing this passage?* (to criticize, to argue, to persuade the reader, to describe, to explain, etc.).
- Practise identifying the topic sentences in paragraphs; this helps to identify the main themes.
- Take notes of the information in a text and use arrows to show how the writer's ideas develop.
- Highlight the cohesive devices used in a text, such as pronoun use, article use, substitution, etc.
- Highlight any words you don't know in a text and practise guessing what they mean from the context. Check your guess in a dictionary.
- Work with a friend to see if you agree on what are the main points and the supporting points in a text. Identify the signpost words that indicate evidence, support, details, examples, or opposing arguments.
- Expand your vocabulary by creating lists of words with their synonyms. Use a thesaurus to find new words with the same or similar meanings. When you learn a new word, find an example of how it is used in context, for example in a learner's dictionary.

Multiple-choice, choose multiple answers

TIP STRIP

Read the question before the options and decide what you need to read for; the words *Which of the following are true* indicate that you are reading for detailed information.

In the test, there are 2–3 tasks. For each task, you read the text on the left of the screen and look at the options on the right of the screen. You click the buttons next to all of the answers you think are correct. The wording in the instructions below is the same as you will see in the actual test. See page 32 for help.

1 Read the text and answer the question by selecting all the correct responses. ***You will need to select more than one response.***

Small, localised enterprises are becoming ever-more imaginative in identifying opportunities to boost tourism for their areas. A more unusual attraction is the Old Man of the Lake, which is the name given to a 9-metre-tall tree stump that has been bobbing vertically in Oregon's Crater Lake since at least 1896. For over one hundred years, it has been largely ignored but recently it has become a must-see item on the list of lake attractions. Since January 2012, tour boats regularly include the Old Man on their sightseeing trips around the lake.

At the waterline, the stump is about 60 centimetres in diameter, and the exposed part stands approximately 120 centimetres above the surface of the water. Over the years, the stump has been bleached white by the elements. The exposed end of the floating tree is splintered and worn but wide and buoyant enough to support a person's weight.

Observations indicated that the Old Man of Crater Lake travels quite extensively, and sometimes with surprising rapidity. Since it can be seen virtually anywhere on the lake, boat pilots commonly communicate its position to each other as a general matter of safety.

Which of the following are true of the Old Man of the Lake according to the passage?

- ○ A It has been a tourist attraction for decades.
- ○ B It is a drifting piece of wood.
- ○ C It is close to the edge of Crater Lake.
- ○ D It is owned by a local businessman.
- ○ E It can quickly move about the lake.
- ○ F It can be a danger to boat users.
- ○ G It is too small for someone to stand on.

TIP STRIP

Use key words in the options to help you find the answers in the text. Key words like *indicates*, *presence*, *good soil* point to the information to be confirmed or contradicted in the text.

TEST 1

READING

2 Read the text and answer the question by selecting all the correct responses. ***You will need to select more than one response.***

To find it, you have to go digging in rainforests, and to the untrained eye, it does not seem special at all – just a thick layer of dark earth that would not look out of place in many gardens. But these fertile, dark soils are in fact very special, because despite the lushness of tropical rainforests, the soils beneath them are usually very poor and thin. Even more surprising is where this dark soil comes from.

'You might expect this precious fertile resource to be found in the deep jungle, far from human settlements or farmers,' says James Fraser, who has been hunting for it in Africa's rainforests. 'But I go looking for dark earth round the edge of villages and ancient towns, and in traditionally farmed areas. It's usually there. And the older and larger the settlement, the more dark earth there is.'

Such findings are overturning some long-held ideas. Jungle farmers are usually blamed not just for cutting down trees but also for exhausting the soils. And yet the discovery of these rich soils – first in South America and now in Africa, too – suggest that, whether by chance or design, many people living in rainforests farmed in a way that enhanced rather than destroyed soils. In fact, it is becoming clear that part of what we think of as lush pure rainforest is actually long-abandoned farmland, enriched by the waste created by ancient humans.

What is significant about the 'dark soil' that the writer is referring to?

- ○ A It indicates the presence of good soil below it.
- ○ B It is not present in rainforests.
- ○ C It has resulted from agricultural activity.
- ○ D It is more common in South America than Africa.
- ○ E It is being found near where humans have lived.
- ○ F It has confirmed what people have believed for a long time.
- ○ G It is less productive than people once thought.

Re-order paragraphs

About the task type

This is a reading task type that tests reading skills. You have to select the single correct order for a set of sentences presented in incorrect order. You have to do 2–3 *Re-order paragraphs* tasks.

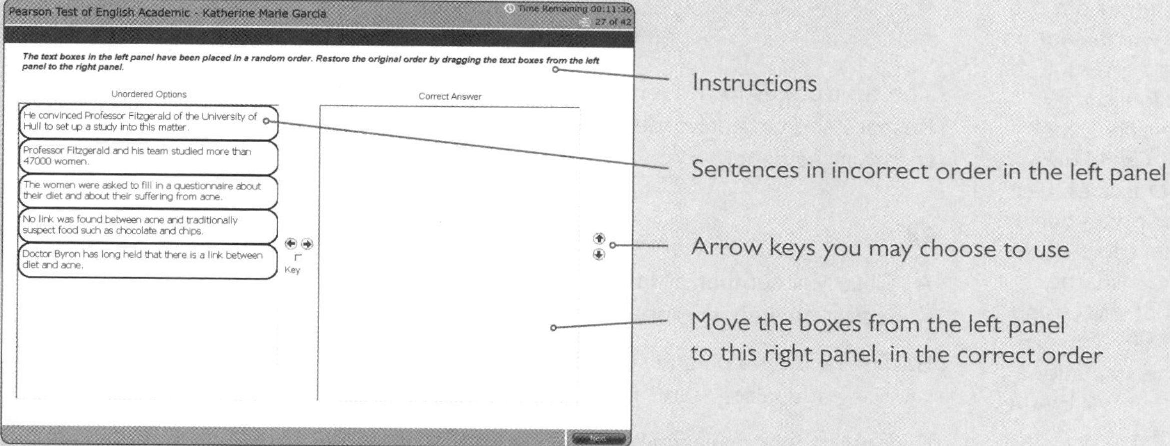

Strategies

Find the topic sentence

- Skim the sentences in the left panel. Look for a sentence that introduces the topic.
- Check that your selected topic sentence 'stands alone', containing no references to any information that must be stated before it.
- Move your topic sentence to the right panel by dragging-and-dropping or using the left/right arrow keys.

Look for the links

- Look for linking words and structures in the other sentences. Look for signal words like *However* or *In addition*, or referencing pronouns replacing nouns already mentioned such as *he* or *it*, or demonstratives such as *this* or *these*. Think about article usage (*a* for first mention, *the* afterwards).
- Use these cohesive markers to put the information in the correct order. Move each sentence to its place in the right panel by dragging-and-dropping or using the arrow keys.

Confirm the order

- Check each sentence. If you change your mind, use the up/down arrow keys or dragging-and-dropping to put the sentence in a different position.
- Read through the sentences in order for one last check, then click 'Next' and move on.

Testing focus Scoring ➤ page 152

Subskills tested

Reading: identifying the topic, theme or main ideas; identifying supporting points or examples; identifying the relationships between sentences and paragraphs; understanding academic vocabulary; understanding the difference between connotation and denotation; inferring the meaning of unfamiliar words; comprehending explicit and implicit information; comprehending concrete and abstract information; classifying and categorizing information; following a logical or chronological sequence of events.

Preparation

- Write a short sentence about a topic. Replace all the nouns with pronouns such as *he*, *she*, *it*, *they*, *them*, etc. Look at the sentence again. Can you see why it is no longer a 'standalone' sentence?
- Look at groups of sentences in magazines or online passages. Highlight the articles *a/an*, *the*. Identify the pattern in article use of first mention/subsequent mention.
- Find short passages of 4–5 sentences in magazines or online. Then:
- Look at the first sentence and ask: *Why is this sentence before the others?*
- Highlight all the words that indicate the cohesion (linking words, pronouns, articles, demonstratives).
- Work with a friend to cut up or re-write the text, moving the sentences into a different order. Exchange texts. Look at each sentence and highlight all the cohesive devices. Use them to re-create the correct order.
- Delete all the referencing pronouns that indicate cohesion. Put the passage aside for a few days, then look at it again and put in the missing words.
- Make a list of signpost words used to show how a text is organized, such as *Firstly, Secondly, However, In addition, On the other hand*, etc.

Re-order paragraphs

TIP STRIP

❶ Read through all the text boxes before you begin. As you do this, note the important words – often nouns that express important ideas, e.g. *collisions*, *erosions*, *rock formations*, *Grand Canyon*, *geological processes*. Use these to help you decide on the main topic of the text; in this case, the formation of the Grand Canyon. Then, you can look for the standalone sentence that will be the first sentence.

❷ Use pronouns and linkers to make connections between sentences and help you work out the correct order, e.g. *It was a time when …*, *As a result, …*, *these …* .

In the test, there are 2–3 tasks. For each task, you drag paragraphs from the left and drop them into the correct order on the right. The wording in the instructions below is the same as you will see in the actual test. See page 35 for help.

The text boxes in the left panel have been placed in a random order. Restore the original order by dragging the text boxes from the left panel to the right panel.

❶

A Clearly, a number of factors have contributed to its remarkable appearance.

B The result is a unique story of land collisions and erosions, and of rising and falling water levels.

C Experts who have analysed the rock formations say that, historically, it goes back nearly two billion years.

D Anyone who has ever visited the Grand Canyon will agree that it is one of the most incredible sights in the world.

E The geological processes that have taken place since then are exposed for everyone to see, not hidden beneath vegetation or a fast-flowing water course.

❷

A It was a time when managers had to take a critical look at every aspect of their production process and make improvements where necessary.

B As a result, some people believe it is now time to re-assess many companies in terms of the standards they agreed to some years ago.

C In the late 1900s, food manufacturers were challenged by the organic community to ensure they were using ingredients that had been produced in natural, healthy ways.

D Whether these systems have been maintained seems questionable, particularly as contracts depend so heavily on efficiency and quick sales.

E Over the last half-century, organic farming has become a driving force in the world's food market.

Reading: Fill in the blanks

About the task type

This is a reading task type that tests reading skills. From the box below a text, you have to select a single correct answer for each gap in the text. You will do 4–5 *Reading: Fill in the blanks* tasks.

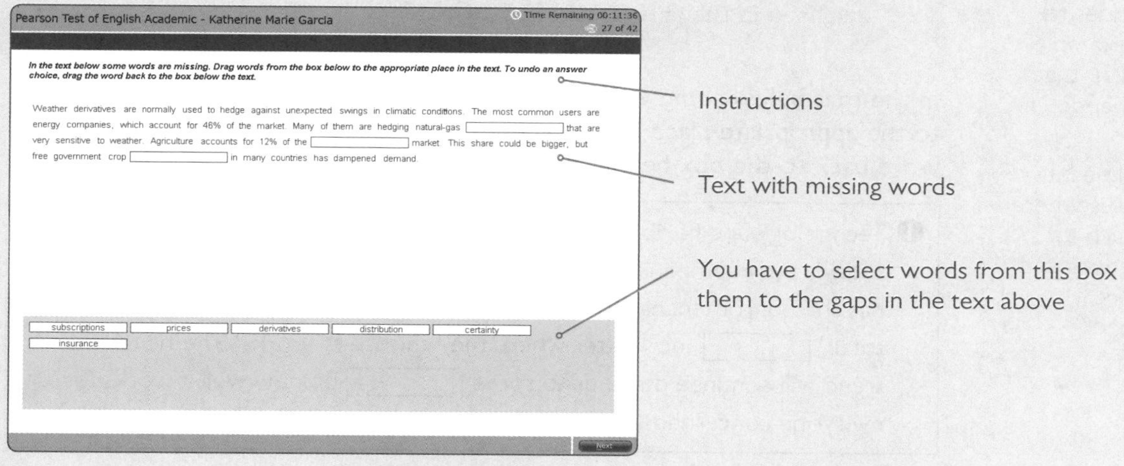

Strategies

Skim the text first

- Skim the gapped text to get an idea of the topic. Ignore the blanks at this point. Look for the key words that carry the meaning.
- If there are words you don't know, read around them to try to guess the meaning from the context.

Identify the correct words

- Look at the words around the first blank and its place in the sentence. Identify the idea being expressed in the sentence, and think what word will create meaning in the context. Use grammar clues to help you decide between possible options.
- Think about collocation: what word often appears with the word before or after the blank?
- Look for possible words in the box at the bottom of the screen, and try each one by dragging it up to the blank in the text. If it fits the meaning and grammar, leave it there. If not, move it back.
- Once you have filled one blank, move to the next. If you cannot do one, don't worry; just move to the next. The more blanks you fill in, the easier the missing ones will be.

Check one last time

- Check each of the 3 unused words to confirm your choices.
- Read through one last time to check the meaning is consistent.

Testing focus Scoring ➤ page 152

Subskills tested

Reading: identifying the topic, theme or main ideas; identifying words and phrases appropriate to the context; understanding academic vocabulary; understanding the difference between connotation and denotation; inferring the meaning of unfamiliar words; comprehending explicit and implicit information; comprehending concrete and abstract information; following a logical or chronological sequence of events.

Preparation

- Improve your general reading skills by reading short texts and summarizing the main ideas. Stop after 2 or 3 sentences and put the ideas you have read into your own words.
- Try to guess the meaning of words you don't know from the context, then check their meaning in a dictionary. Use a thesaurus to expand your vocabulary with synonyms for the word, and look for examples of how to use the new words, for example in a learner's dictionary.
- Expand your knowledge of collocation (words that frequently occur together, such as *difficult decision*). Keep a diary of collocations you find in your reading and revise them regularly. This will help you to recognize the best word for a blank.
- Make your own collocation lists. Take a common word such as *pollution* and add to it any words you would expect to see it used with, such as *water pollution, air pollution, urban pollution*. Expand this list by taking the words you have found and adding different collocations, for example, with *water* you can put *water pollution, water sports, water supply, water shortage, clean water, fresh water,* etc.
- Work with a friend to delete some of the words that carry meaning from short texts. Exchange texts and try to guess the missing word, with and without having a list to choose from.

Reading: Fill in the blanks

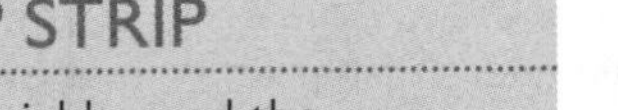

TIP STRIP

1. Quickly read the paragraph first. Then use grammar clues to help you. For example, *have had* tells you that a plural noun is needed in the first gap.
2. Some gaps will be in common phrases where collocations, such as between adjectives and nouns like *a wide* ______, can help you find the answer.

In the test, there are 4–5 tasks. For each task, you drag the words at the bottom of the text and drop them into the correct space in the text. The wording in the instructions below is the same as you will see in the actual test. See page 37 for help.

In the text below some words are missing. Drag words from the box below to the appropriate place in the text. To undo an answer choice, drag the word back to the box below the text.

1 Technology and flexible work [1] ______ have had a significant impact on today's busy companies. In terms of productivity, it seems the [2] ______ has shifted from managing employees in the workplace to monitoring their total [3] ______, no matter where they choose to work. Whether this trend will continue depends to some [4] ______ on how well it works for everyone concerned.

focus | deals | way | practices | selling | output | extent

2 Elephants have a very [1] ______ communication system, which helps them maintain their close [2] ______ bonds. When they are near each other, they use verbal and visual signals to express a wide [3] ______ of emotions. As they move further [4] ______, they use less common, rumbling [5] ______ that can be heard over two kilometres away.

distant | variety | family | ranging | apart | sounds | complex | round

TEST 1

READING

TIP STRIP

3 Use pronoun references to help you complete the gap. For example, *these huge* refers back to *wind farms*. Select a word from the box that completes the description.

4 You can use your knowledge of grammar and collocation. For example, in Gap 3, choose the verb from the box that collocates with *contribution*.

In the text below some words are missing. Drag words from the box below to the appropriate place in the text. To undo an answer choice, drag the word back to the box below the text.

3 People are naturally concerned about the polluting 1 _____ of energy sources such as oil or coal. But are wind farms the 2 _____? With their enormous rotating blades, these huge 3 _____ are becoming more commonplace in certain 4 _____ of the world. Yet for some people, they are an unwelcome 5 _____ of the landscape.

machines | product | sight | feature | answer | regions | damages | effects

4 Professional astronomers, 1 _____ their amateur counterparts, have no particular interest in the aesthetic quality of their photographs. What 2 _____ to them is the contribution their images can 3 _____ to research, and to the 4 _____ of data scientists in their field 5 _____ for research purposes.

make | equipped | unlike | matters | use | collection | put | concerns

TEST 1

READING

Reading & writing: Fill in the blanks

About the task type

This is a multiple-choice reading task type that tests reading and writing skills. You select one correct word from a list to fill each blank in a text. You will do 5–6 *Reading & writing: Fill in the blanks* tasks.

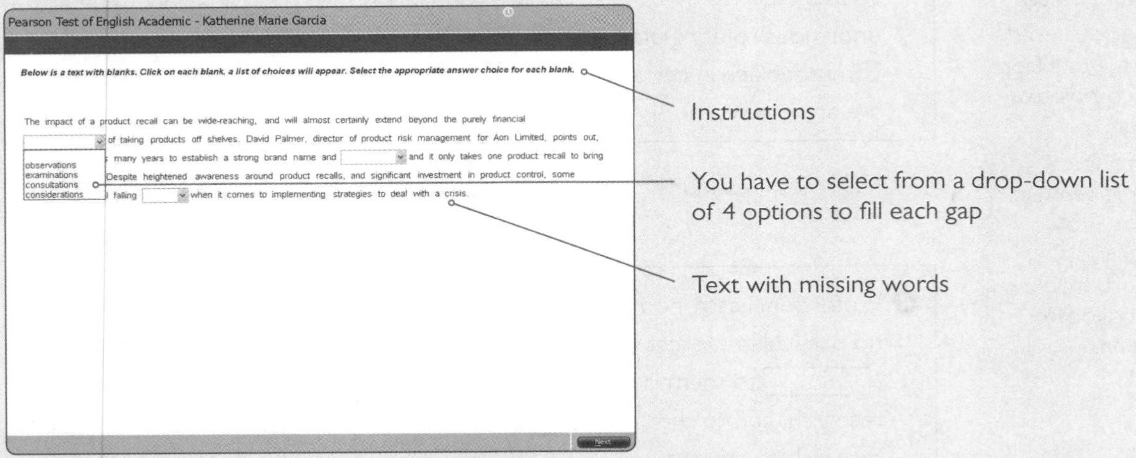

Strategies

Read the text through

- Read the whole text through once for the overall meaning. Then, re-read the sentence with the first blank and think what word would create meaning in the context. Look at the sentence grammar to decide what is needed, e.g. noun, past tense verb, adjective.
- Click on the first blank. From the drop-down list, select the one that will create meaning and is grammatically correct.
- Repeat for the other blanks.

Use your language knowledge

- Think about collocation: what word often appears with the word before or after the blank?
- Consider word form: should the word be the noun form, the verb form, or the adjective form? For example: *allocation, allocate, allocated, allocating*.
- Read the sentence with each word in turn: which one makes the best meaning in context?

Check for grammar and meaning

- Fill each blank in turn. If you cannot do one, leave it and return later. The more blanks you fill, the clearer the text will become.
- When you have finished, check each selection for correct grammar. If it is a verb, is the tense correct? Is it the right form of the word?
- Click 'Next' and move on.

Testing focus Scoring ➤ page 152

Subskills tested

Reading: identifying the topic, theme or main ideas; identifying words and phrases appropriate to the context; understanding academic vocabulary; understanding the difference between connotation and denotation; inferring the meaning of unfamiliar words; comprehending explicit and implicit information; comprehending concrete and abstract information; following a logical or chronological sequence of events.

Writing: using words and phrases appropriate to the context; using correct grammar.

Preparation

- Improve your general reading skills by reading short texts and summarizing the main ideas. Look at the sentence structure and trace the verb tense patterns and the clause structure.
- Revise your knowledge of grammar and word order. Use a grammar book with gap-fill quizzes to practise choosing the grammatically correct word for each gap.
- When reading texts, try to guess the meaning of words you don't know from the context, then check their meaning in a dictionary. Use a thesaurus to expand your vocabulary with synonyms for the word, and look for examples of how to use the new words, for example in a learner's dictionary.
- Expand your knowledge of collocation (words that frequently occur together, such as *difficult decision*). Keep a diary of collocations that you find in your reading and revise them regularly. This will help you to recognize the best word for a blank.
- Notice the discourse structure when you read, how the writers use cohesive devices to indicate the progression of what they are saying. This will help you to choose the correct option based on understanding the construction of a text.
- Work with a friend to delete words such as verbs and nouns from texts. Exchange texts and try to predict what the missing words should be.

Reading & writing: Fill in the blanks

TIP STRIP

1. Read the text quickly before you start to get an overall understanding of the content and decide on the main idea or topic. This will help you choose words with the right meaning.
2. Note any small words like prepositions that come after the gap. These will help you rule out some options, for example, in Gap 2, only one of the options has the correct meaning and can be followed by *in*.

In the test, there are 5–6 tasks. For each task, you have a text with several gaps. You select the correct answer for each gap from the drop-down list on the screen. The wording in the instructions below is the same as you will see in the actual test. See page 40 for help.

Below is a text with blanks. Click on each blank, a list of choices will appear. Select the appropriate choice for each blank.

1 It would be very hard to imagine life without electricity. Most of the appliances and machines that are used in homes, offices and factories are powered by electricity and this equipment [1] _____ people's overall quality of life. For that reason, the wider provision of electricity supplies is a critical factor in reducing global poverty [2] _____ . To meet the needs of users around the world, the global consumption of coal has risen more quickly [3] _____ 2000 than any other fuel. For countries that do not have their own supply of natural energy resources, coal has become an essential [4] _____ of producing power. On a global scale, coal is currently used to fire power stations and produces 40% of global electricity. This [5] _____ is very likely to increase, and predictions are that by 2030 coal will fuel 44% of the world's electricity.

1	A helps improving	B helps to improve	C help improve	D help improved
2	A levels	B ranks	C stages	D degrees
3	A for	B in	C since	D at
4	A means	B factor	C aspect	D course
5	A total	B sum	C volume	D figure

2 People are living longer and this longevity is good news for sales teams. It results in a much more [1] _____ customer base for them to work from. Why we are living longer is not the issue for anyone [2] _____ in drawing up plans to market a product. What they focus on is the fact that there are now more age groups to target, which means that a sales pitch can be re-worked a number of times to more exactly fit each one. For example, [3] _____ referring simply to 'adults', there are now 'starting adults', 'young adults' and 'established adults'. [4] _____ markets no longer talk about 'children', but tend to refer to a fuller range of categories that includes 'kids', 'tweens', 'pre-teens' and 'teenagers'. We now have a very diverse population in terms of age, and that can only be a [5] _____ for business.

1	A usual	B precise	C right	D honest
2	A linked	B mixed	C concerned	D involved
3	A rather than	B by	C even when	D while
4	A While	B Similarly	C Even	D Really
5	A desire	B favour	C bonus	D promise

Below is a text with blanks. Click on each blank, a list of choices will appear. Select the appropriate answer choice for each blank.

TIP STRIP

3 Think about whether you need a countable or uncountable noun. For example, there is no article before Gap 1 and, although all the options have similar meanings, only one is used with *reference* to form an uncountable noun phrase.

4 Look at what comes after the gap. For example, in Gap 2, only one option in this set can be followed by an infinitive verb form.

3 Experts have waited a considerable amount of time for this much-needed book. Now we have a new and very thorough survey of wetland plant species. The content is extensive and totally up-to-date and as reference 1 ______, it represents extremely good value. In addition to the editors, there are 35 well-chosen contributors who have put in a tremendous amount of work to 2 ______ the reader with maps and indexes, and colourful photographs. The plant descriptions are straightforward, yet scholarly, and flicking through the pages, 3 ______ the writers' passion for the subject. Each of the eight sections has an overview, 4 ______ current concerns and future conservation plans. Despite a few gaps and the occasional unsatisfactory illustration, this handbook will remind botanists and specialists of the importance of protecting the country's plant life. 5 ______ person interested in the topic, whether student or hardened expert, will find it indispensable.

1	A piece	B report	C book	D material
2	A manage	B assist	C contribute	D hand
3	A it can sense	B one sense	C you can sense	D he senses
4	A highlighting	B focusing	C bringing	D involving
5	A The other	B Any one of	C Every	D All

4 At the moment, there are between six and seven thousand languages in the world. According to linguists, fifty percent of these are in danger 1 ______ extinct. The speed of language loss has accelerated over the past few decades because businesses that need to communicate with a range of people from other cultures 2 ______ to employ more widely used languages, such as English, Chinese, or Spanish. This attitude is understandable, but it means that many local languages are dying out before anyone 3 ______ the opportunity to study them. According to linguists, some of these languages could reveal a great 4 ______ of useful information about language learning and cognitive development. In addition, a local language that has been built on the local culture contains words and phrases that express that culture; lose the language and you arguably may lose the culture, too. And finally, historians will 5 ______ that a language contains evidence of a region's history and should, for that reason alone, be preserved.

1	A have become	B to become	C of becoming	D became
2	A prefer	B fancy	C select	D must
3	A have	B would have	C having had	D has had
4	A size	B deal	C capacity	D load
5	A speak	B tell	C argue	D explore

Below is a text with blanks. Click on each blank, a list of choices will appear. Select the appropriate answer choice for each blank.

5 Bamboo is a favoured plant among architects and designers because of its incredible strength and durability. One Colombian architect [1] ______ to it as nature's steel, but in many respects it is even better than steel: it is lighter and more flexible, and these [2] ______ make it the ideal building material in areas that suffer earthquakes and severe weather patterns. Construction workers in places such as Hong Kong rely on bamboo scaffolding whatever the [3] ______ of the tower block they may be working on; over a billion people around the world live in a home that is made of bamboo; and China [4] ______ the plant for thousands of years. The only drawback to this remarkable product is the cost of transporting it. So for those [5] ______ live in cooler regions of the world, the enormous advantages of this natural building material are less accessible.

1	A implies	B mentions	C indicates	D refers
2	A abilities	B qualities	C talents	D values
3	A mass	B top	C summit	D height
4	A has cultivated	B cultivate	C cultivates	D had cultivated
5	A which	B may	C who	D are

TIP STRIP

5 Use reference words such as *this, these, it,* etc. to help you make the correct choice. For example, in Gap 2, *these* refers back to the idea of being *lighter* and *more flexible*. Only one option is the correct group noun.

Overview: Listening

Part 3 of the PTE Academic test is Listening. This part tests your ability to understand spoken English in an academic environment. It also tests your ability to understand a variety of accents, both native and non-native.

The table shows what you will see in the test, which you will take on a computer. When practising with this book, you will have to write your written answers in the book, your notebook or on your own device, and you could record your spoken answers on your own device, for example a mobile phone.

Part 3: Listening				
Listening (total time 45–57 minutes)				
Task type	Number of tasks	Task description	Skills assessed	Text/ Recording length
Summarize spoken text	2–3	After listening to a recording, write a summary of 50–70 words.	listening and writing	60–90 seconds
Multiple-choice, choose multiple answers	2–3	After listening to a recording, answer a multiple-choice question on the content or tone of the recording by selecting more than one response.	listening	40–90 seconds
Fill in the blanks	2–3	The transcription of a recording appears on screen with several blanks. While listening to the recording, type the missing words into the blanks.	listening and writing	30–60 seconds
Highlight correct summary	2–3	After listening to a recording, select the paragraph that best summarizes the recording.	listening and reading	30–90 seconds
Multiple-choice, choose single answer	2–3	After listening to a recording, answer a multiple-choice question on the content or tone of the recording by selecting one response.	listening	30–60 seconds
Select missing word	2–3	After listening to a recording, select the missing word or group of words that completes the recording.	listening	20–70 seconds
Highlight incorrect words	2–3	The transcription of a recording appears on screen. While listening to the recording, identify the words in the transcription that differ from what is said.	listening and reading	15–50 seconds
Write from dictation	3–4	After listening to a recording of a sentence, type the sentence.	listening and writing	3–5 seconds

Each recording is played only once. You may take notes using the Erasable Noteboard Booklet and pen, and use these notes as a guide when answering the tasks.

With the exception of *Summarize spoken text*, listening task types are not timed individually. You can refer to the timer in the upper right-hand corner of the computer screen, *Time Remaining*, which counts down the time remaining for the Listening part.

Summarize spoken text

About the task type

This is a long-answer listening task type that tests listening and writing skills. You have to summarize the key points in a short lecture, in 50–70 words. You will do 2–3 *Summarize spoken text* tasks.

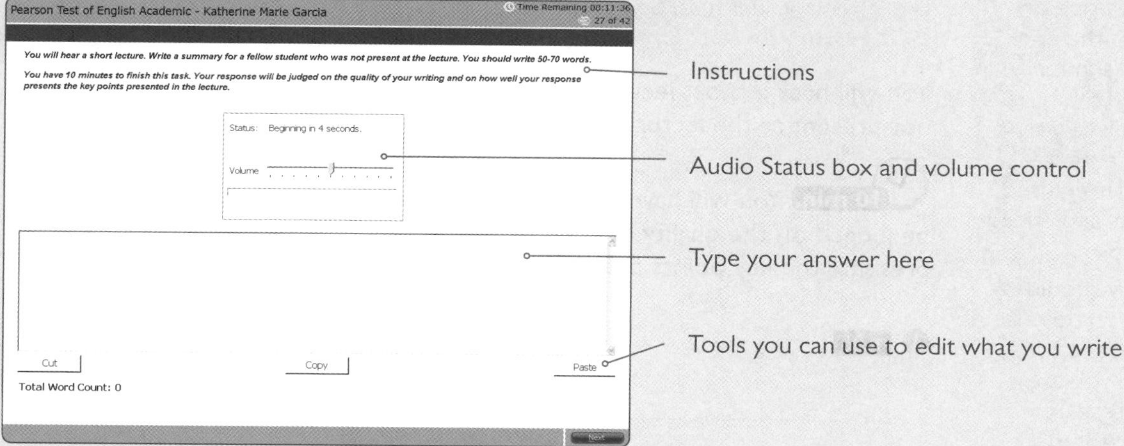

Pearson Test of English Academic - Katherine Marie Garcia
Time Remaining 00:11:36
27 of 42
You will hear a short lecture. Write a summary for a fellow student who was not present at the lecture. You should write 50-70 words.
You have 10 minutes to finish this task. Your response will be judged on the quality of your writing and on how well your response presents the key points presented in the lecture.
Status: Beginning in 4 seconds.
Volume
Cut
Copy
Paste
Total Word Count: 0
Next
Instructions
Audio Status box and volume control
Type your answer here
Tools you can use to edit what you write

Strategies

Be ready

- The Audio Status box will count down from 12 seconds and the audio will begin.
- Be ready to take notes on the Erasable Noteboard Booklet.

Take notes as you listen

- As you listen, take notes of the main and supporting ideas.
- Don't try to write down everything you hear. Use key words, abbreviations, symbols and arrows to capture the most important ideas and to indicate how the ideas are organized. Effective note-taking will ensure that your summary has all the main points.
- When the recording stops, look at your notes while the audio is fresh in your mind. Plan how you will present the information.

Write your summary

- When the audio stops, you have 10 minutes to write your summary.
- Use your notes to summarize all the main points and add as many supporting details or examples as you can. Top marks will be gained if all relevant aspects of the audio are mentioned.
- Keep to the word limit of 50–70 words, or you will lose marks.
- Save 2 minutes at the end to check your work for grammar and spelling. Mistakes will lose marks.
- After 10 minutes, the screen will stop responding. Click 'Next'.

Testing focus Scoring ➤ page 153

Subskills tested

Listening: identifying the topic, theme or main ideas; summarizing the main idea; identifying supporting points or examples; identifying a speaker's purpose, style, tone or attitude; understanding academic vocabulary; inferring the meaning of unfamiliar words; comprehending explicit and implicit information; comprehending concrete and abstract information; classifying and categorizing information; following an oral sequencing of information; comprehending variations in tone, speed and accent.

Writing: writing a summary; writing under timed conditions; taking notes whilst listening to a recording; communicating the main points of a lecture in writing; organizing sentences and paragraphs in a logical way; using words and phrases appropriate to the context; using correct grammar; using correct spelling; using correct mechanics.

Preparation

- Develop your own techniques for rapid note-taking. Decide on your own abbreviations and symbols and practise using them so they become automatic.
- Find podcasts of lectures with a transcript. Highlight the signal words that indicate the main points and the examples, or evidence, or opposing arguments, then listen for them in the audio to help you understand.
- Find podcasts of lectures online. Listen to 30 seconds of a lecture, noting the key words, then stop the audio and write a sentence that summarizes the main points of what you heard. Repeat this twice until you have listened to 90 seconds. Then, join your sentences into a summary of 50–70 words. Practise until you can listen to 90 seconds without stopping the audio. Summarize 2 or 3 short lectures and time yourself at 10 minutes for each summary.
- Practise writing grammatically correct sentences. Simple sentences that communicate meaning will score better than complex sentences with errors. The best responses use concise, correct sentences that communicate meaning clearly.

Summarize spoken text

TIP STRIP

1 Your grammar, vocabulary and spelling should be accurate. Leave one or two minutes at the end to check your summary. Have you used the right tenses? Have you started each sentence with a capital letter, used commas in lists and ended with a full stop?

2 Your summary should include the main point(s) and important supporting points. When you are summarizing research or an experiment, note down the key stages, paying less attention to examples or minor details.

In the test, there are 2–3 tasks. For each task, you listen to the audio then type your summary into the box on the screen. The wording in the instructions below is the same as you will see in the actual test. See page 45 for help.

You will hear a short lecture. Write a summary for a fellow student who was not present at the lecture. You should write 50–70 words.

10 min. You will have 10 minutes to finish this task. Your response will be judged on the quality of your writing and on how well your response presents the key points presented in the lecture.

1 ▸ 25

....

....

....

....

....

....

2 ▸ 26

....

....

....

....

....

....

Multiple-choice, choose multiple answers

About the task type

This is a multiple-choice listening task type that tests listening skills. More than one response is correct in answer to a question about a lecture. You will do 2–3 *Multiple-choice, choose multiple answers* tasks.

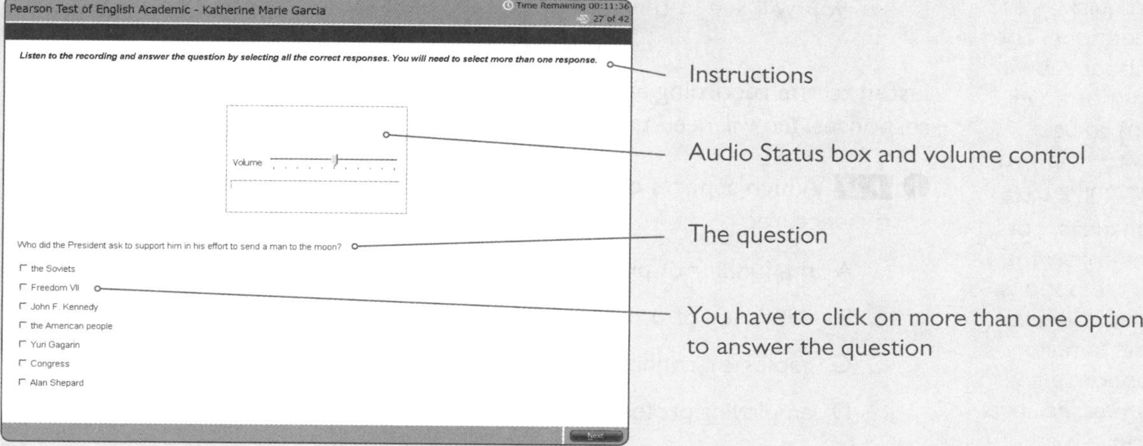

Strategies

Read and think ahead

- Read the question and skim the options before the audio begins. This will tell you what the topic is as well as what information you are listening for. It could be the main ideas, the writer's goals or attitudes, some detailed information, or inferences.

Stay focused

- Keep your attention on the audio. Take notes of key words if you wish, to help you remember the information you hear.
- As you listen, be aware of the development of the speaker's ideas so you can recognize the core information.
- Listen for the general flow of ideas and don't worry if you miss or don't know individual words.
- After the audio finishes, eliminate options that contain incorrect information or have information that was not mentioned.
- Answer the question by clicking on more than one option or on their checkboxes.

Confirm your choice

- After you have chosen the options, check again that each of the other options is incorrect. If you change your mind, click on the option again to de-select it then click on the correct option.
- Be aware of the time and don't spend too much time on one task.

Testing focus Scoring ➤ page 154

Subskills tested

Listening: any of the following depending on the task: identifying the topic, theme or main ideas; identifying supporting points or examples; identifying specific details, facts, opinions, definitions or sequences of events; identifying a speaker's purpose, style, tone or attitude; identifying the overall organization of information and connections between pieces of information; inferring the context, purpose or tone; inferring the meaning of unfamiliar words; predicting how a speaker may continue.

Preparation

- Listen to lectures you find on the web and stop the audio about every minute to answer this question: *What points has the speaker made?* Summarize the main points.
- Listen to lectures you find on the web and stop the audio about every minute to answer this question: *What is the speaker doing here?* (introducing, criticizing, summarizing, persuading, describing, etc.).
- Take notes of the information in a short extract from a lecture and use arrows to show how the speaker's ideas develop.
- Practise activating relevant vocabulary: listen to the opening sentence of a lecture, then stop the lecture and make a list of all the words on that topic that you expect to hear. Circle each one as you listen to the lecture and add other words to your list.
- Find podcasts of lectures with a transcript. Highlight the signal words that indicate the main points and the examples, or evidence, or opposing arguments, then listen for them in the audio. Highlight any words you don't know in the transcript and practise guessing what they mean from the context. Check your guess in a dictionary.
- Expand your vocabulary by creating lists of words with their synonyms. Use a thesaurus to find new words with the same or similar meanings. Look for the words in context, for example in a learner's dictionary.

Multiple-choice, choose multiple answers

In the test, there are 2–3 tasks. For each task, you listen to the audio then click the buttons next to all of the answers you think are correct. The wording in the instructions below is the same as you will see in the actual test. See page 47 for help.

Listen to the recording and answer the question by selecting all the correct responses. *You will need to select more than one response.*

1 ▶ 27 Which aspects of subway construction will the speaker talk about in this lecture?

- ○ A the funding of projects
- ○ B the speed of trains
- ○ C geological conditions
- ○ D employing professionals
- ○ E public approval
- ○ F passenger movement

2 ▶ 28 According to the speaker, which of the following measures helped reduce community problems in Brickendon?

- ○ A allowing residents to patrol the area
- ○ B interviewing residents about the problems
- ○ C organizing regular community meetings
- ○ D giving families financial support
- ○ E identifying hotspots for crime
- ○ F removing litter from the streets

TIP STRIP

1 Before you listen, decide on the main focus of the question and quickly read through the options. The question is about subway construction (not travel or relocation) so use those words to help you focus your listening.

2 Listen for the ideas, not just words or synonyms for words in the options. If you just match words without understanding the whole option, e.g. *residents*, *families*, *hotspots* you may choose the wrong answers.

Fill in the blanks

About the task type

This is a listening task type that tests listening and writing skills. You have to listen to a recording and write the missing words in a transcription of the recording. You will do 2–3 *Fill in the blanks* tasks.

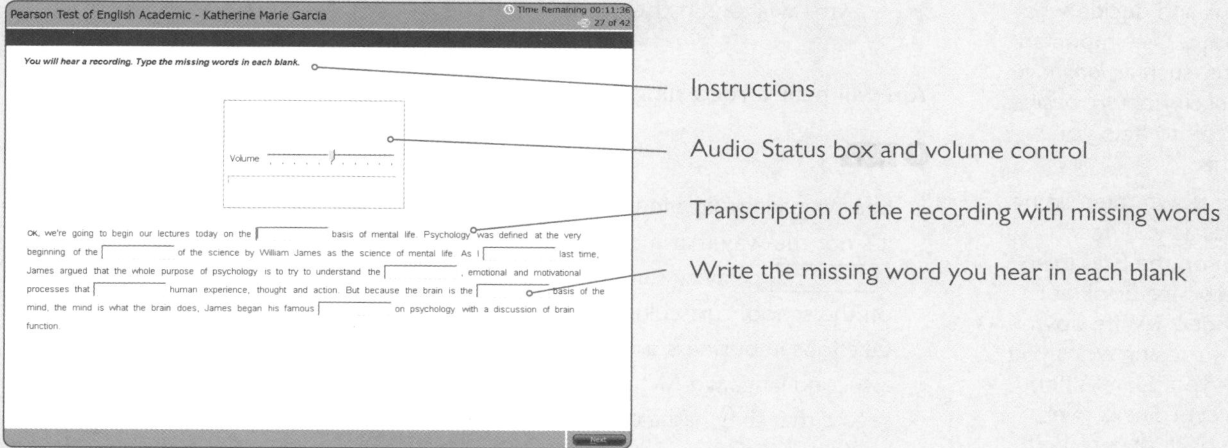

Strategies

Be ready

- Quickly skim the text to gain a general idea of the topic.
- Be ready to write each missing word on your Erasable Noteboard Booklet as you hear each one, or type directly into each blank.
- The Audio Status box will count down from 7 seconds and the audio will then begin.

Write what you hear

- As you hear each missing word during the recording, write or type the word quickly and be ready for the next one. Do not check your spelling at this point.
- Follow the speaker in the transcription so you do not miss a word. Do not get behind.
- Keep writing or typing each missing word until the audio stops.

Check and type

- After the audio stops, read the sentence that has the first missing word and confirm that the word you wrote makes sense.
- Continue for each blank. Type carefully and check your spelling each time. Incorrect spelling will score zero for that blank.
- Use grammar clues to make sure you type the correct form of the word (noun, verb, adjective, etc.).
- Read through one last time for meaning to confirm each word and check your spelling. Click 'Next' to move on.

Testing focus Scoring ➤ page 154

Subskills tested

Listening: identifying words and phrases appropriate to the context; understanding academic vocabulary; comprehending explicit and implicit information; following an oral sequencing of information.
Writing: writing from dictation; using words and phrases appropriate to the context; using correct grammar; using correct spelling.

Preparation

- Practise matching the written form of a word to the sound. Listen to a podcast of a lecture and stop the audio every 10 seconds. Write down the last word you heard, then play that part again to check that the word you wrote makes sense in the sentence.
- Check the pronunciation of any new words you learn by using a dictionary with the words recorded. Make sure you know where the stress falls within the word.
- Confirm the spelling of new words as you learn them. Practise typing new words in lists; this will also help to familiarize you with a QWERTY keyboard (the type of English-language keyboard used in PTE Academic).
- Ask a friend to read short sentences to you from a magazine. Type the sentences you hear on your computer with the spell-checker turned off. Look at what you have written: are there any misspelled words? Run the spell-checker through the sentence to see if you were right.
- Create a word bank for new words with as many forms of the word listed as you can find, such as the noun, verb, adjective and adverb form of words, e.g. *education* (n), *educate* (v), *educated* (adj). You can add synonyms, antonyms and collocations to your word bank to expand your vocabulary. Add to your word bank every day.
- If you hear part of a word, you can work out what form the word must be and how to spell it using grammar and context clues. Use a grammar book with gap-fill quizzes to practise choosing the grammatically correct word for each gap.

Fill in the blanks

TIP STRIP

1. Quickly read the text before the recording begins and decide what it is about. Use important nouns, such as *languages*, *school curriculum*, *business* and *CVs* to help you do this.
2. Note down the missing words as you hear them on the Erasable Noteboard Booklet provided. Write down every missing word you think you hear. When the recording is over, use your notes to help you decide on the correct spelling.

In the test, there are 2–3 tasks. For each task, there is a text with several gaps. You type the correct answer for each gap into the box in the text. The wording in the instructions below is the same as you will see in the actual test. See page 49 for help.

You will hear a recording. Type the missing words in each blank.

1 ▶ 29

Learning a language in the classroom is never easy and, quite [1] ______, it's not the way that most people would choose to learn if they had other [2] ______. Having said that, there are plenty of reasons for keeping languages on the school curriculum. For one thing, a fair number of students go on to take jobs in business and commerce that require a [3] ______ knowledge of a second language. When you talk to young [4] ______ in top companies, it seems that they had a career plan from the start; they were motivated to find additional things to put on their CVs – and of course language is one of those added, but [5] ______ extras.

2 ▶ 30

The assignment that I'm going to set for the holiday period is one that we've given students for a number of years. It's quite [1] ______ and will allow you to get out and about – it's no good being shut up in your rooms all the time! It does have a written [2] ______, too. Um, basically it's a data gathering exercise and there are two choices with regard to how you [3] ______ the data. We'll go through those in a moment. I'm also going to give you a link to an internet site that is – well it's critical that you [4] ______ this before you do anything, as it provides a lot of guidance on data presentation, both in terms of how you plot it – its diagrammatic form and also its [5] ______, which has to be clear.

Highlight correct summary

About the task type

This task type tests listening and reading skills. You will listen to a short lecture then identify the correct summary of the information you have heard. You will do 2–3 *Highlight correct summary* tasks.

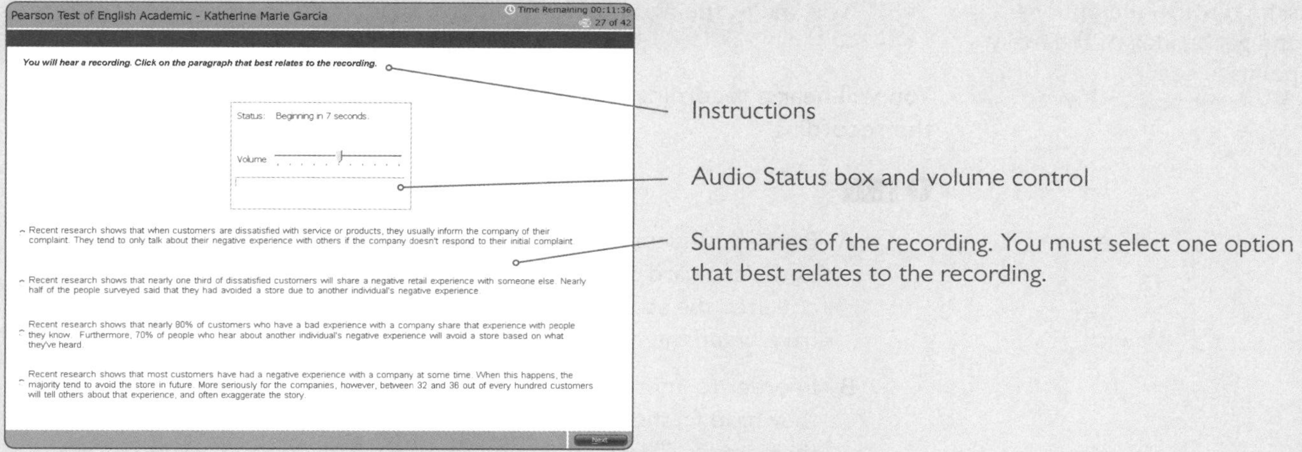

Pearson Test of English Academic - Katherine Marie Garcia
Time Remaining 00:11:36
27 of 42
You will hear a recording. Click on the paragraph that best relates to the recording.
Status: Beginning in 7 seconds.
Volume
Recent research shows that when customers are dissatisfied with service or products, they usually inform the company of their complaint. They tend to only talk about their negative experience with others if the company doesn't respond to their initial complaint
Recent research shows that nearly one third of dissatisfied customers will share a negative retail experience with someone else. Nearly half of the people surveyed said that they had avoided a store due to another individual's negative experience.
Recent research shows that nearly 80% of customers who have a bad experience with a company share that experience with people they know. Furthermore, 70% of people who hear about another individual's negative experience will avoid a store based on what they've heard.
Recent research shows that most customers have had a negative experience with a company at some time. When this happens, the majority tend to avoid the store in future. More seriously for the companies, however, between 32 and 36 out of every hundred customers will tell others about that experience, and often exaggerate the story.
Instructions
Audio Status box and volume control
Summaries of the recording. You must select one option that best relates to the recording.

Strategies

Be ready

- Use the 10 seconds as the audio counts down to skim the 4 summaries quickly to gain an idea of the topic. You will not have time to read thoroughly.
- Be ready to listen and take notes of key ideas using your Erasable Noteboard Booklet.

Listen and take notes

- As you listen, take notes of the main and supporting ideas.
- Don't try to write down everything you hear. Use key words, abbreviations, symbols and arrows to capture the most important ideas.
- Note any data given in support of an argument, or any implications suggested by the speaker.
- Do not try to read the summaries as you listen. Each one is 40–60 words, so there is too much information. Focus on listening.

Match notes and summary

- When the audio stops, use your notes to select the correct option.
- First, eliminate any options that contain incorrect information.
- Eliminate any options that focus on only one aspect of the information, or that contain information that was not mentioned at all.
- Check the remaining option against your notes to confirm that it covers all aspects of the lecture. Select that option and move on.

Testing focus Scoring ➤ page 154

Subskills tested

Listening: identifying the topic, theme or main ideas; identifying supporting points or examples; understanding academic vocabulary; inferring the meaning of unfamiliar words; comprehending explicit and implicit information; comprehending concrete and abstract information; classifying and categorizing information; following an oral sequencing of information; comprehending variations in tone, speed and accent.

Reading: identifying supporting points or examples; identifying the most accurate summary; understanding academic vocabulary; inferring the meaning of unfamiliar words; comprehending concrete and abstract information; classifying and categorizing information; following a logical or chronological sequence of events; evaluating the quality and usefulness of texts.

Preparation

- Develop your own techniques for rapid note-taking. Decide on your own abbreviations and symbols and practise using them so they become automatic.
- Practise skimming sets of summaries using the practice tests in this book. After 10 seconds, use the words you notice to predict the probable content of the lecture.
- Find podcasts of lectures with a transcript. Highlight the signal words that indicate the main points and the examples, or evidence, or opposing arguments, then listen for them in the audio. Underline words in the transcript that the speaker highlights with stress or intonation; these help to indicate the key points.
- Listen to 30 seconds of a lecture, noting the key points, then stop the audio and write a sentence that summarizes the main information you heard. Repeat this twice until you have listened to 90 seconds. Then, join your sentences into a summary; practice in *writing* summaries will help you to *recognize* a summary. Practise until you can listen to 90 seconds without stopping the audio, then produce a complete summary.

Highlight correct summary

TIP STRIP

Use the ten seconds before the recording begins to skim through the options and get an idea of the main points in each.

In the test, there are 2–3 tasks. For each task, you listen to the audio then click the button next to the summary you think is correct. The wording in the instructions below is the same as you will see in the actual test. See page 51 for help.

You will hear a recording. Click on the paragraph that best relates to the recording.

1 ▸ 31

○ A Business students are finding it increasingly difficult to get employment, as the standard of law courses has declined since 2007. Employers have criticized the schools for adopting unsatisfactory teaching methods, and have urged them to ensure students get higher grades.

○ B In order to improve the chances of their students obtaining jobs after they have finished their courses, some business schools are adjusting their grades. These adjustments are being made to all grades awarded since 2007 but instead of benefiting the students it is, in some instances, having the opposite effect.

○ C Some business schools have realized that their grading system has been inaccurate since 2007 and are currently making changes to correct the errors. Students' grades are being revised, and employers have welcomed this move as it means that they will be able to employ better qualified students.

○ D Since 2007, the education of business students has been improving but this has not been reflected in the grades that they are achieving. Business schools have been under pressure from employers to ensure that the grades that students are achieving match their abilities far better than in recent years.

You will hear a recording. Click on the paragraph that best relates to the recording.

TIP STRIP

Listen for the signposts that indicate the main ideas. Speakers use words and phrases like the first thing I wanted to talk about, on the one side, on the other side to help listeners understand the flow of their ideas.

2 ▶ 32

- ○ A Many existing buildings in city centres, such as Perth are being cleared to make way for modern developments. Although this is improving the visual impact of the city, it is causing difficulties in areas where there is not enough space to accommodate the expanding population.
- ○ B Developers in Perth and other parts of Western Australia are suggesting that it would be better to build much-needed homes within the city centre, as this would be more affordable for local people. It would also make transportation to and from jobs and shops cheaper and quicker.
- ○ C Cities like Perth in Western Australia are experiencing a rapid growth in urban development, and the current trend is to expand into surrounding regions. Although some people think this is more cost effective than building within cities, others believe it's having a harmful effect on the environment in these areas.
- ○ D The housing shortage in Perth is being addressed by encouraging people to move to other cities in Western Australia where there is more space to develop new housing and infrastructure. This will benefit people struggling to find accommodation and also avoid having to develop on bushland.

Multiple-choice, choose single answer

About the task type

This is a multiple-choice listening task type that tests listening skills. You have to select a single answer to a question about a lecture. You will do 2–3 *Multiple-choice, choose single answer* tasks.

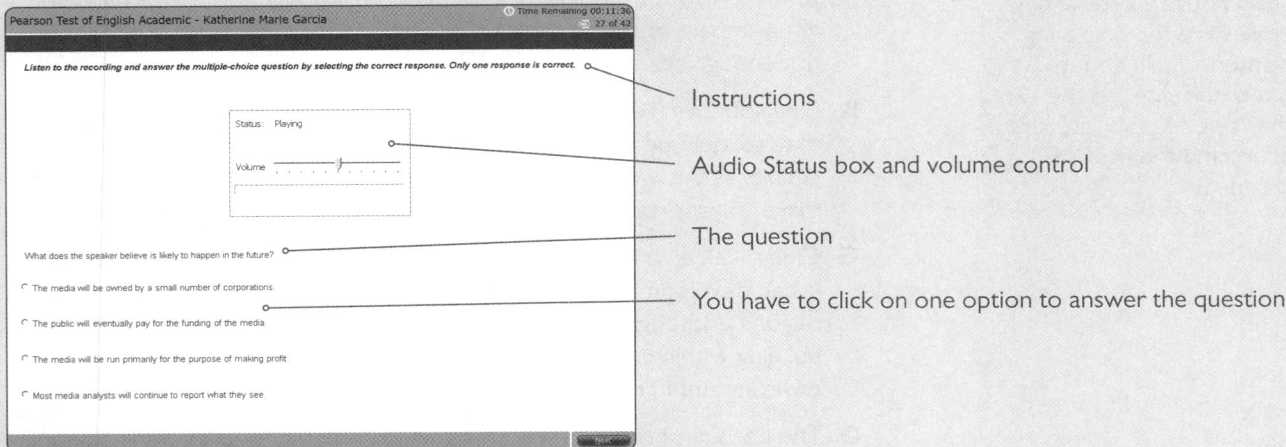

Strategies

Read and think ahead

- Read the question and skim the options before the audio begins. This will tell you what the topic is as well as what information you are listening for. It could be the main idea, the writer's goal or attitude, some detailed information, or an inference that can be drawn.

Stay focused

- Keep your attention on the audio. Take notes of key words if you wish, to help you remember the information you hear.
- As you listen, be aware of the development of the speaker's ideas so you can recognize the core information.
- Listen for the general flow of ideas and don't worry if you miss or don't know individual words.
- After the audio finishes, eliminate options that contain incorrect information or have information that was not mentioned.
- Answer the question by clicking on one option or on its radio button ○ .

Confirm your choice

- After you have chosen the option, check again that each of the other options is incorrect. If you change your mind, click on the option again to de-select it then click on the correct option.
- Be aware of the time and don't spend too much time on one task. Click 'Next' and move on.

Testing focus Scoring ➤ page 154

Subskills tested

Listening: any of the following depending on the task: identifying the topic, theme or main ideas; identifying supporting points or examples; identifying specific details, facts, opinions, definitions or sequences of events; identifying a speaker's purpose, style, tone or attitude; identifying the overall organization of information and connections between pieces of information; inferring the context, purpose or tone; inferring the meaning of unfamiliar words; predicting how a speaker may continue.

Preparation

- Listen to lectures you find on the web and stop the audio about every minute to answer this question: *What points has the speaker made?* Summarize the main points.
- Listen to lectures you find on the web and stop the audio about every minute to answer this question: *What is the speaker doing here?* (introducing, criticizing, summarizing, persuading, describing, etc.).
- Take notes of the information in a lecture and use arrows to show how the speaker's ideas develop.
- Practise activating relevant vocabulary: listen to the opening sentence of a lecture, then stop the lecture and make a list of all the words on that topic that you expect to hear. Circle each one as you listen to the lecture and add other words to your list.
- Find podcasts of lectures with a transcript. Highlight the signal words that indicate the main points and the examples, or evidence, or opposing arguments, then listen for them in the audio. Highlight any words you don't know in the transcript and practise guessing what they mean from the context. Check your guess in a dictionary.
- Expand your vocabulary by creating lists of words with their synonyms. Use a thesaurus to find new words with the same or similar meanings. When you learn a new word, find an example of how it is used in context, for example in a learner's dictionary.

Multiple-choice, choose single answer

In the test, there are 2–3 tasks. For each task, you listen to the audio then click the button next to the answer you think is correct. The wording in the instructions below is the same as you will see in the actual test. See page 54 for help.

Listen to the recording and answer the multiple-choice question by selecting the correct response. *Only one response is correct.*

1 ▶ 33 What is the speaker's main focus?

- ○ A reasons why Americans have relocated
- ○ B the growth in the American population
- ○ C the expansion of suburban towns
- ○ D trends in where Americans live

2 ▶ 34 What do the speakers feel about early views on malaria?

- ○ A They were understandable at the time.
- ○ B They resulted in unnecessary illness.
- ○ C They have contributed to current findings.
- ○ D They will be remembered in the future.

TIP STRIP

1 Read the question carefully before you read the options so that you know what you need to listen for. This question is about the main focus so you need to listen to the whole recording and decide which option best describes the overall idea.

2 The words *early views* are important in this question – they tell you that you are listening for opinions on something specific. Listen to what the speakers say about these.

Select missing word

About the task type

This task type tests listening skills. From a set of options, you have to predict what word(s) a speaker will say, based on contextual clues in a recording. You will do 2–3 *Select missing word* tasks.

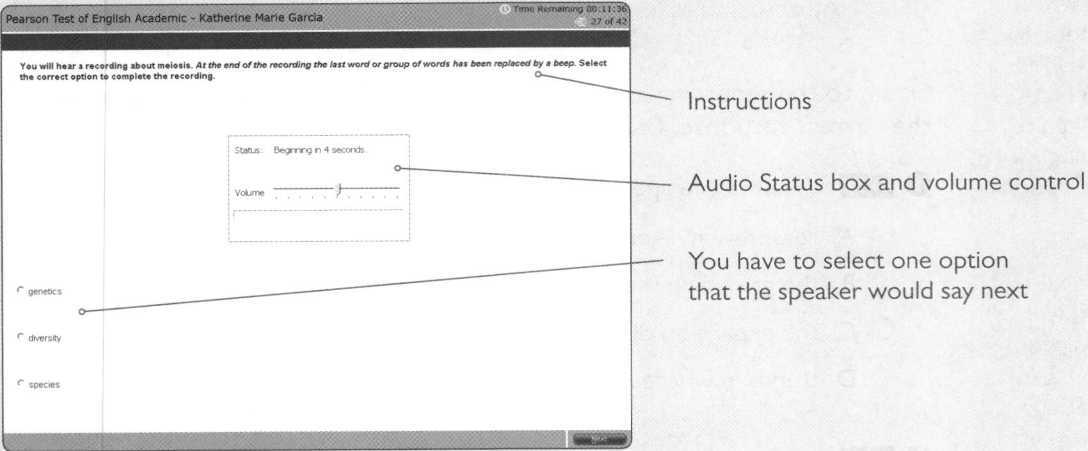
Pearson Test of English Academic - Katherine Marie Garcia
Time Remaining 00:11:36
27 of 42
You will hear a recording about meiosis. At the end of the recording the last word or group of words has been replaced by a beep. Select the correct option to complete the recording.
Status: Beginning in 4 seconds.
Volume
genetics
diversity
species
Next
Instructions
Audio Status box and volume control
You have to select one option that the speaker would say next

Strategies

Be ready

- The instructions tell you the topic of the recording. As the Audio Status box counts down from 7 seconds, think what vocabulary you might hear.
- Skim the options quickly to gain an idea of the aspect of the topic the speaker might talk about.
- Be ready to focus on what you hear, and nothing else.

Listen attentively

- As you listen, make a mental map of what you are hearing. Do not take notes – it is more important to listen for the development of the speaker's ideas.
- Listen for any signal words the speaker might use to tell you the direction of the talk, e.g. presenting opposite arguments, describing something in detail, supporting a claim, etc.
- Don't worry about any words you don't understand. Focus on the overall ideas.

Predict the ending

- Be aware of the blue bar in the Audio Status box. This shows you when the recording is coming to an end so you will be ready to suggest the word or phrase that has been replaced by a beep.
- As soon as the recording stops, think what would come next and scan the options for the most similar word or phrase. Select it.

Testing focus Scoring ➤ page 155

Subskills tested

Listening: identifying the topic, theme or main idea; identifying words and phrases appropriate to the context; understanding academic vocabulary; inferring the meaning of unfamiliar words; comprehending explicit and implicit information; comprehending concrete and abstract information; following an oral sequencing of information; predicting how a speaker may continue; forming a conclusion from what a speaker says; comprehending variations in tone, speed and accent.

Preparation

- Work with a friend. Find 2 magazine articles and take turns to read out a short paragraph to each other, stopping before the final word or phrase. Try to guess what word or phrase will complete the paragraph.
- Develop your skills of predicting the ideas you will hear. Listen to 20 seconds of a lecture, then stop the audio and say what ideas you think the speaker will talk about next. Play on and check your prediction. Repeat this with longer recordings.
- Find podcasts of lectures with a transcript. Highlight the signal words that indicate the main points and the examples, or evidence, or opposing arguments, then listen for them in the audio. Look at the way these signal words will tell you the direction of the lecture and what the speaker is likely to say next.
- Find podcasts of lectures with a transcript. Play the lecture, stopping the audio about every 30 seconds. Predict what words the speaker will say next, then check the transcript. Compare the written form of the words with how they sound in the lecture.
- Practise predicting what vocabulary you will hear in lectures on different topics. Play the first sentence or two of a short lecture, then make a list of the words and phrases you expect to hear. Play the lecture to check how many words from your list you hear.
- Expand your vocabulary of academic words in context. Keep a record of new words you learn.

Select missing word

TIP STRIP

1. If the options are phrases, read each one quickly while the audio counts down from seven seconds, and decide what you need to listen for. If the answer is A, you should hear a comparison related to writers; B, an overview of how popular something has been; C, reference to how something has changed over time; and D, a description of something that facilitates reading.
2. If the options are single words, consider their meaning and whether they are linked in any way. These options all describe the quality of something. You will need to listen for which quality is discussed by the speaker.

In the test, there are 2–3 tasks. For each task, you listen to the audio then click the button next to the words you think complete the audio. The wording in the instructions below is the same as you will see in the actual test. See page 56 for help.

1 ▶ 35 You will hear a recording about fiction writing. *At the end of the recording the last word or group of words has been replaced by a beep.* Select the correct option to complete the recording.

- ○ A suits some writers better than others
- ○ B is becoming more popular
- ○ C has changed over time
- ○ D makes reading easier

2 ▶ 36 You will hear a recording about biology. *At the end of the recording the last word or group of words has been replaced by a beep.* Select the correct option to complete the recording.

- ○ A complex
- ○ B unreal
- ○ C confusing
- ○ D invisible

Highlight incorrect words

About the task type

This task type tests listening and reading skills. As you listen to a recording, you have to identify words in a transcription that differ from what you hear. You will do 2–3 *Highlight incorrect words* tasks.

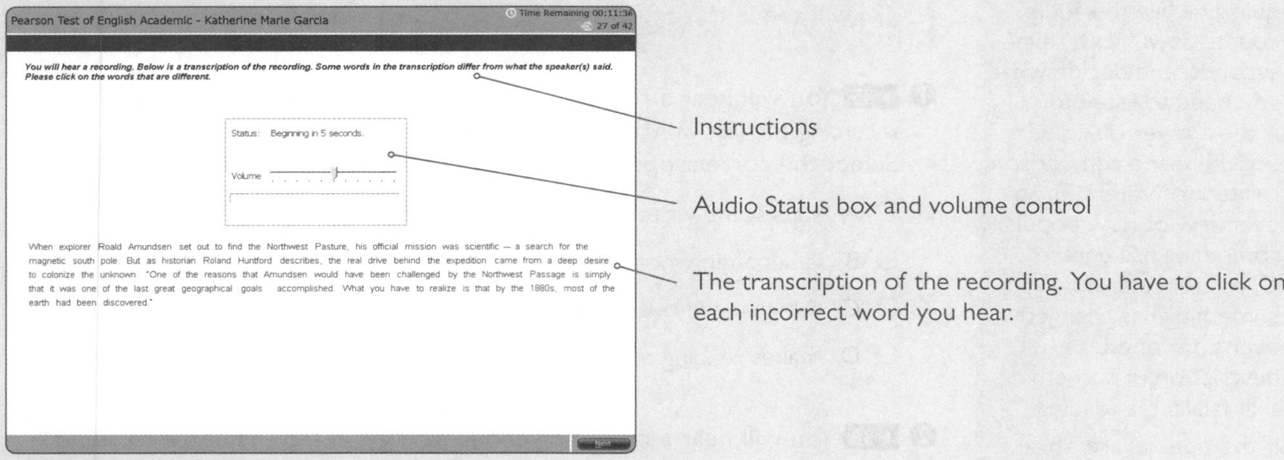

STRATEGIES

Strategies

Be ready

- Use the 10 seconds before the recording begins to skim the transcription, to familiarize yourself with the topic.
- Move your cursor to the start of the transcription before the audio begins.

Follow the recording

- As soon as the recording begins, move your cursor along each line following the speaker's voice.
- Think how each word you are reading will sound and as soon as you hear a different word, click on the incorrect word.
  The word you have clicked on will be highlighted and will remain highlighted until you click on it again.
- Keep up with the speaker. Do not stop to think about whether your selection was correct or incorrect. If you lose your place it will be difficult for you to catch up and you may miss some words that you should have selected.

Try not to change your mind

- Do not change your mind unless you feel very sure you have made a mistake. Success in this task type depends on real-time decisions.
- Do not guess. You will lose marks for words you click on that were in fact the correct word that was in the recording. There are up to 7 'errors' in each transcription.

Testing focus Scoring ➤ page 155

Subskills tested

Listening: identifying errors in a transcription; understanding academic vocabulary; following an oral sequencing of information; comprehending variations in tone, speed and accent.

Reading: understanding academic vocabulary; following a logical or chronological sequence of events; reading a text under timed conditions; matching written text to speech.

Preparation

- When you learn a new word, use a dictionary that has the words recorded so you can check both the pronunciation of the sounds and where the word stress falls.
- Listen to the way the final sound in one word links to the first sound in the next when people speak. Be prepared for this when you follow the transcription.
- Remember that when people speak, they group the words into meaningful chunks. Be prepared to follow the rhythm of the recording as you read the transcription.
- Find podcasts of lectures with a transcript. In the transcript, highlight the words or phrases you think will be stressed and the words or phrases that will be unstressed or weak. Listen to the podcast in sections and check if you were right.
- In podcasts of lectures with a transcript, highlight in a short section of the transcript all the key words that carry the meaning and think how they are pronounced. Decide where the word stress falls within each word. Check in a dictionary. Then, play the lecture and listen to how the speaker pronounces each of the words you highlighted.
- Listen to podcasts by speakers with different English accents so that you become familiar with the way different speakers pronounce words, especially where they place the word stress, e.g. (UK): *re<u>search</u>*/(US): *<u>re</u>search*. Some consonants will also be different, such as in *schedule*.

Highlight incorrect words

TIP STRIP

TIP STRIP

1. You will not have time to read the transcription carefully before the recording begins, but you will have time to skim it quickly. As you do this, decide what the general topic of the paragraph is. This will help you follow the ideas as you listen.
2. As you listen, follow the words with the cursor on screen (or your pencil in this book) and click on (or mark) any words that sound different from the transcript.

In the test, there are 2–3 tasks. For each task, you listen to the audio and follow the words in the text on the screen. You click on the words that are different on the screen and the audio. The wording in the instructions below is the same as you will see in the actual test. See page 58 for help.

You will hear a recording. Below is a transcription of the recording. *Some words in the transcription differ from what the speaker said.* Please click on the words that are different.

1 ▶ 37 Transcription:

It seems we now know more about outer space than we do about the Earth's core. This is because temperatures are so great at the centre of the Earth that human beings have not been able to take a close look at it. However, new techniques of analysis may soon change all that. The seismic waves formed by earthquakes and volcanic eruptions penetrate the Earth's layers at different speeds. It is now hoped that by studying these waves, scientists will be able to make new findings and solve some of the mysteries of the inside structure of the Earth.

2 ▶ 38 Transcription:

Many species of birds cover long miles during their seasonal migration to warmer climates. But how successful are they, and do birds that get lost on their route ever survive to find their way back? Much research has been done into how birds navigate and the results show that age is a significant reason. Young birds usually just carry on, if they lose their migratory path, and thus fail to achieve their destination, whereas older, more experienced birds will generally be able to find their first route and continue successfully on their journey.

Write from dictation

About the task type

This task type tests listening and writing skills. You have to write a sentence that you will hear once only, in a recording that lasts 3 to 5 seconds. You will do 3–4 *Write from dictation* tasks.

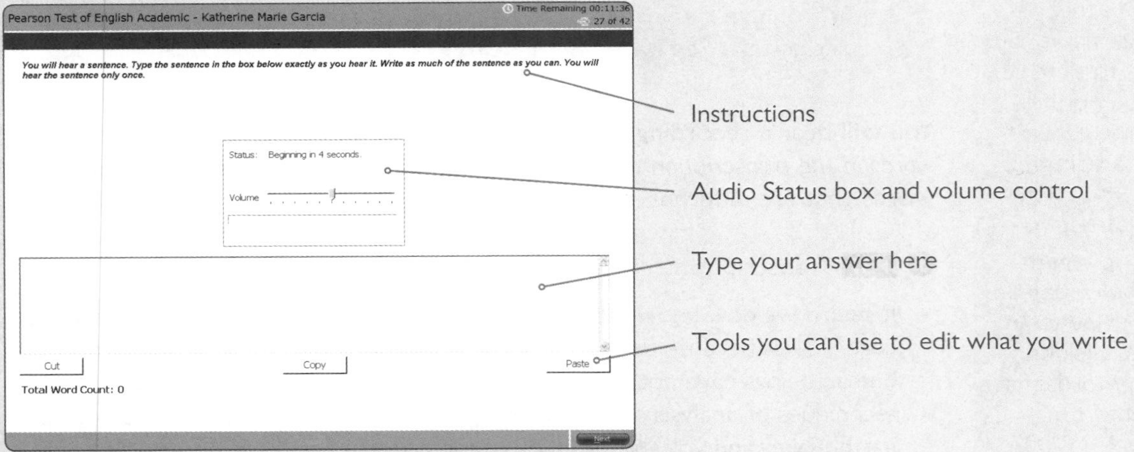

Pearson Test of English Academic - Katherine Marie Garcia
Time Remaining 00:11:36
27 of 42
You will hear a sentence. Type the sentence in the box below exactly as you hear it. Write as much of the sentence as you can. You will hear the sentence only once.
Status: Beginning in 4 seconds.
Volume
Cut
Copy
Paste
Total Word Count: 0
Next
Instructions
Audio Status box and volume control
Type your answer here
Tools you can use to edit what you write

Strategies

Be ready

- The Audio Status box will count down from 7 seconds. Focus so that you do not miss any words.
- If you prefer to write the sentence by hand first, be ready to write on your Erasable Noteboard Booklet.
- If you prefer to type directly on the screen, place your cursor in the box on the screen.

Focus on meaning

- When the audio begins, focus on the meaning of the sentence. This will help you to remember it.
- Write or type the content words (nouns, verbs, adjectives and adverbs). Leave the minor words (prepositions, articles) for now.
- Write or type as quickly as you can. Don't worry about spelling at this point. Start writing as soon as the dictation begins and don't stop to check your writing yet.

Construct and check

- Immediately after the recording stops, write or type as much of the sentence as you can.
- Go over the sentence and use your knowledge of grammar, word form and word order to add any words you missed out (e.g. prepositions, articles).
- Check the spelling of every word. Check for verb endings and plurals. Marks are awarded for every correct word spelled correctly. Then click 'Next'.

Testing focus Scoring ➤ page 155

Subskills tested

Listening: understanding academic vocabulary; following an oral sequencing of information; comprehending variations in tone, speed and accent.

Writing: writing from dictation; using correct spelling.

Preparation

- Decide in advance whether you are going to write the sentence by hand or write directly on the screen. Once you have decided which method you prefer, practise dictations using it and don't change your mind on the test day.
- Practise guessing how to spell words you don't know. Write down words you hear in the media, in advertisements, the news, interviews. Try to confirm the spelling of the word you heard using a dictionary.
- Revise your knowledge of the normal spelling conventions. Make a list of words you have trouble spelling, especially words with *ie* or *ei*, or doubled consonants such as *mm*, *ll*, *pp*, *ss*.
- Make a list of words with similar pronunciation but different spelling and different meaning, such as *affect/effect*, *except/accept*, *no/know*, *fair/fare*. Check the meaning of each one.
- Create a word bank for new words with as many forms of the word listed as you can find, such as the noun, verb, adjective and adverb form of words, e.g. *evidence* (n), *evident* (adj), *evidently* (adv). In the test, you may miss part of a word so you may have to work out which form is needed and spell it correctly.
- Practise writing sentences with correct word endings, such as *-ed* endings on past tenses and -s endings on plurals and present tenses.
- Listen to podcasts by speakers with different English accents to become familiar with them.
- Remember that this is the final task type in the test. Be aware of the time remaining in Part 3 so that you have enough time to attempt every question. It is better to try every task than to spend too much time on a task you have finished.

Write from dictation

TIP STRIP

1. As you listen, write all the words that you hear on your Erasable Noteboard Booklet. After the recording, write the sentence in the response box.
2. When you write the sentence, write the words you hear and do not paraphrase. You will gain marks for each correct word spelled correctly.
3. Try to spell words correctly and check the grammar before you click on 'Next'. Don't miss endings, such as *-ed* on past verb forms, *-ly* on adverbs or *-s* on plurals.

In the test, there are 3–4 tasks. For each task, you listen and type the sentence you hear into the box on the screen. The wording in the instructions below is the same as you will see in the actual test. See page 60 for help.

You will hear a sentence. Type the sentence in the box below exactly as you hear it. Write as much of the sentence as you can. You will hear the sentence only once.

1 ▶ 39

....

....

....

2 ▶ 40

....

....

....

3 ▶ 41

....

....

....

TEST 2

TEST 2

SPEAKING

Read aloud

TIP STRIP

Read first to get an idea of the overall meaning of the text, e.g. Text 1 is about statistics. Look for the words that contain key information; these are usually stressed, e.g. *statistics*, *economy*, *population*, *environment*, *visible*, *accessible*, *robust*.

Practise saying any difficult words, e.g. *statistics*, *statistically literate*. Think about where your voice will rise, fall and pause.

In the test, there are 6–7 tasks. For each task, you read the text aloud into the microphone. The wording in the instructions below is the same as you will see in the actual test. See page 12 for help.

40 sec. **Look at the text below. In 40 seconds, you must read this text aloud as naturally and as clearly as possible. You have 40 seconds to read aloud.**

1. Statistics reflect vital information about the economy, the well-being of the population, and the environment. Society relies on statistics being visible, accessible and robust, and on statistically literate people making the best use of the information to determine future action. Statistical literacy, then, is the ability to accurately understand, interpret and evaluate the data that inform these issues.

2. Housing fulfils the basic needs that people have for security, privacy and shelter. While the adequacy of housing is an important component of individual well-being, housing also has great impact on the nation's economy, with its influence on investment levels, interest rates, building activity and employment.

3. Being physically active benefits people's health significantly, including reducing the risk of some chronic conditions, helping to control weight, and improving mental health. In recent decades, there has been a decline in physical activity because more people work in offices rather than in manual jobs.

4. Students who wish to take a break from their studies will need to put in an application for Leave of Absence. If your application is successful, you will be notified via email. At the end of your Leave of Absence, you must re-enrol at Student Services and in the subjects you intend to study.

5. There are a number of tests available which can suggest if a person is telling the truth, but knowing which ones are accurate is not easy. A newly created test is claimed to be the most accurate yet in lie detection. However, questions have been raised about its accuracy and ethics.

6. A student exchange program complements formal education, while promoting tolerance, maturity and independence – all highly sought after qualities in today's competitive job market. Living in the host country, not as a tourist or guest but as a member of the community, is what makes the experience both challenging and rewarding.

Repeat sentence

TIP STRIP

Focus on the meaning of the sentence and the key words, e.g. in Sentence 1: *students, extension, tutors.* Notice the stressed words and where the speaker's voice rises and falls, and imitate this when you speak. Does the speaker's voice go up or down at the end of the sentence?

If you take notes, don't try to write every word. Note the key words using abbreviations, e.g. *sts, ext, tut.*

In the test, there are 10–12 tasks. For each task, you listen and repeat the sentence you hear into the microphone. The wording in the instructions below is the same as you will see in the actual test. See page 14 for help.

▸ 42–51  15 sec. You will hear a sentence. Please repeat the sentence exactly as you hear it. You will hear the sentence only once.

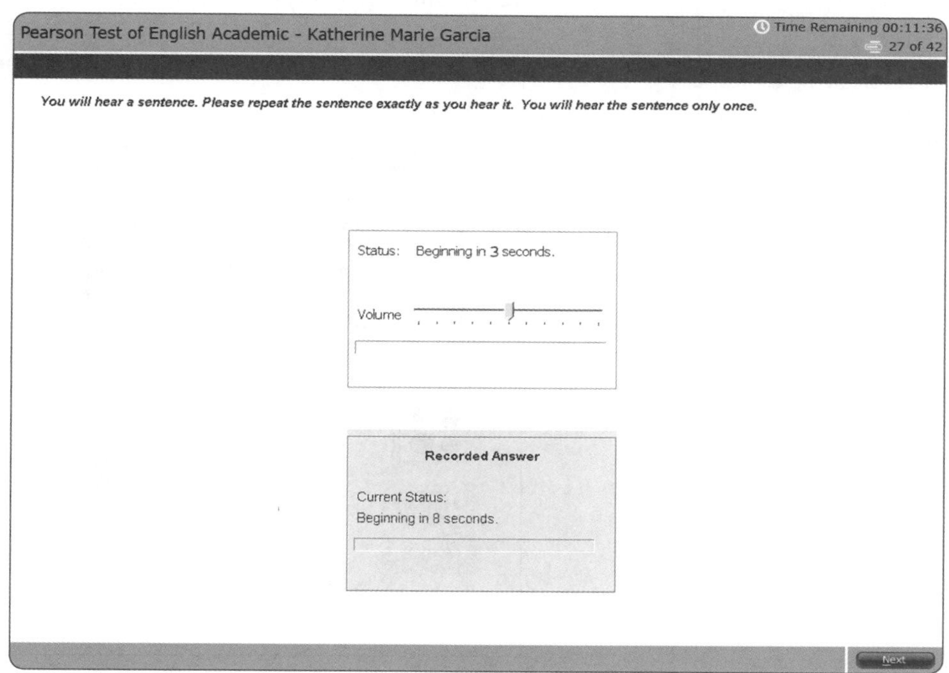

Repeat sentence: Each question is displayed on a new screen.

TEST 2 SPEAKING

Describe image

TIP STRIP

Look at the title of the image. This helps you to begin with a general statement about the information, and then you can describe the major features. In Question 1, the plan shows student accommodation, and the major features are the overall size and number of rooms, their location and their contents.

In the test, there are 6–7 tasks. For each task, you look at the image and describe it into the microphone. The wording in the instructions below is the same as you will see in the actual test. See page 16 for help.

1 **40 sec.** Look at the plan below. In 25 seconds, please speak into the microphone and describe in detail what the plan is showing. You will have 40 seconds to give your response.

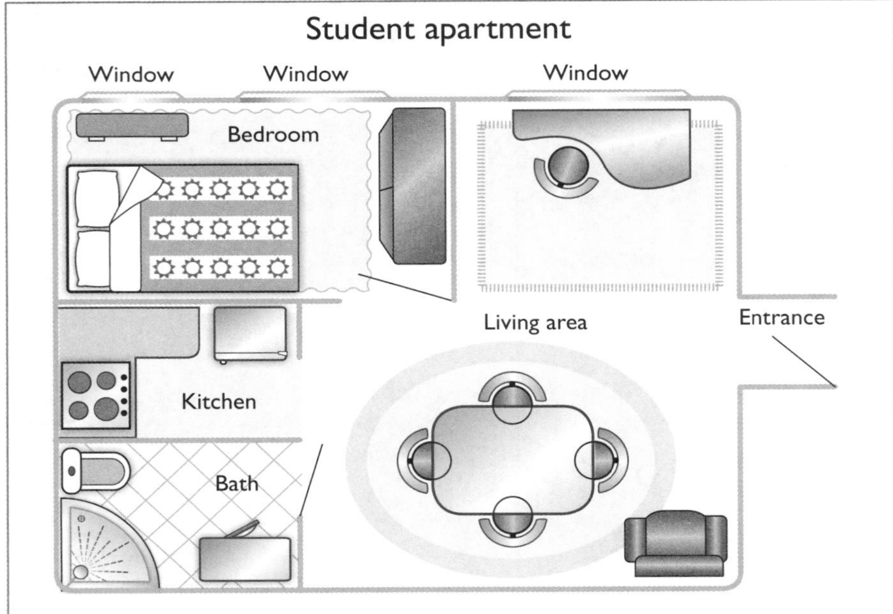

2 **40 sec.** Look at the graph below. In 25 seconds, please speak into the microphone and describe in detail what the graph is showing. You will have 40 seconds to give your response.

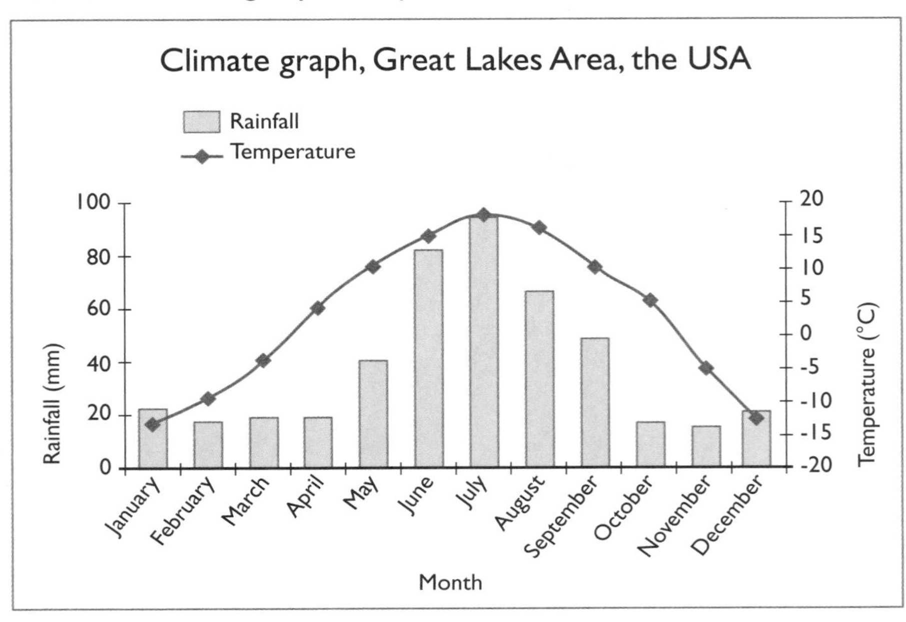

3 40 sec. Look at the graph below. In 25 seconds, please speak into the microphone and describe in detail what the graph is showing. You will have 40 seconds to give your response.

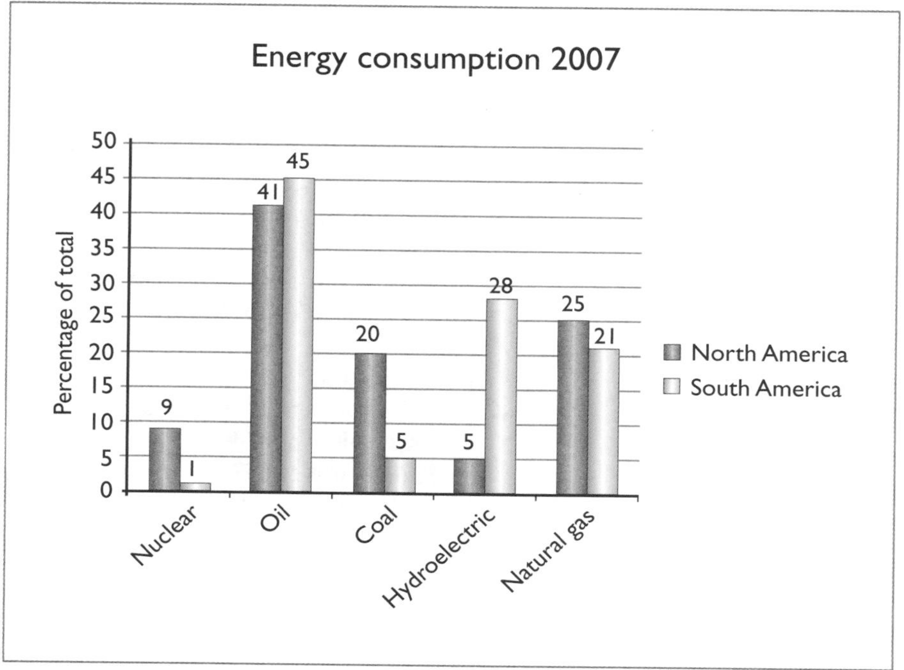

4 40 sec. Look at the table below. In 25 seconds, please speak into the microphone and describe in detail what the table is showing. You will have 40 seconds to give your response.

Language college timetable, week 1

	Day 1	Day 2	Day 3	Day 4	Day 5	Day 6	Day 7
9 a.m. to 12 noon	Tour of college	English language class	English language class	English language class	Full day activities: *Examples: tennis, films, games, surfing*	Weekend with Homestay families	Weekend with Homestay families
	Welcome by Head of college and Morning tea	English language class	English language class	English language class			
1 p.m. to 4 p.m.	English language class	Social activity on site	Excursion to local attraction	Visit to Junior School classroom			
	Social activity on site	Social activity on site		Social activity on site			

5 40 sec. Look at the graph below. In 25 seconds, please speak into the microphone and describe in detail what the graph is showing. You will have 40 seconds to give your response.

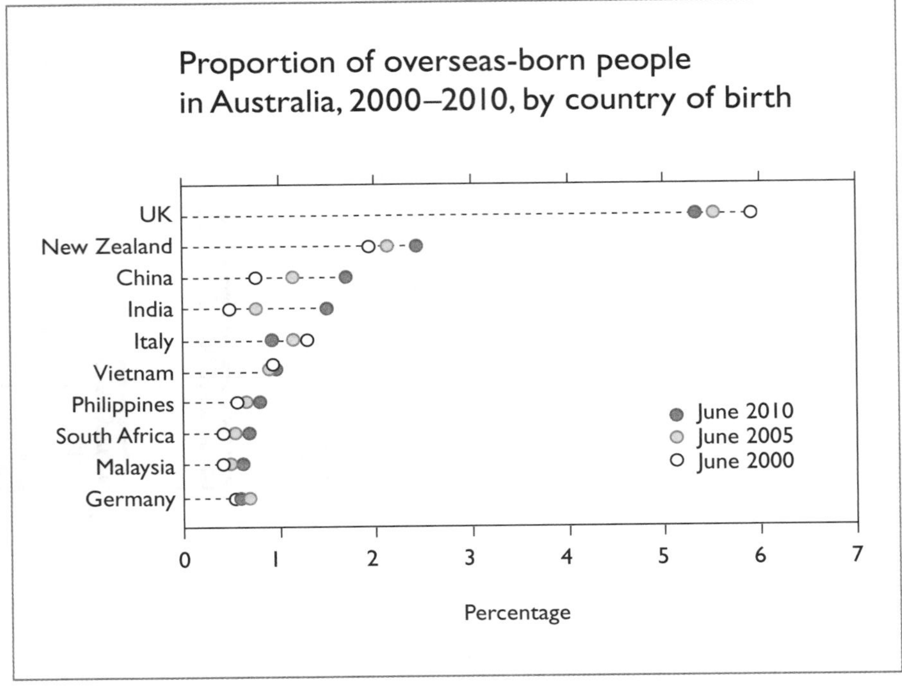

6 40 sec. Look at the diagram below. In 25 seconds, please speak into the microphone and describe in detail what the diagram is showing. You will have 40 seconds to give your response.

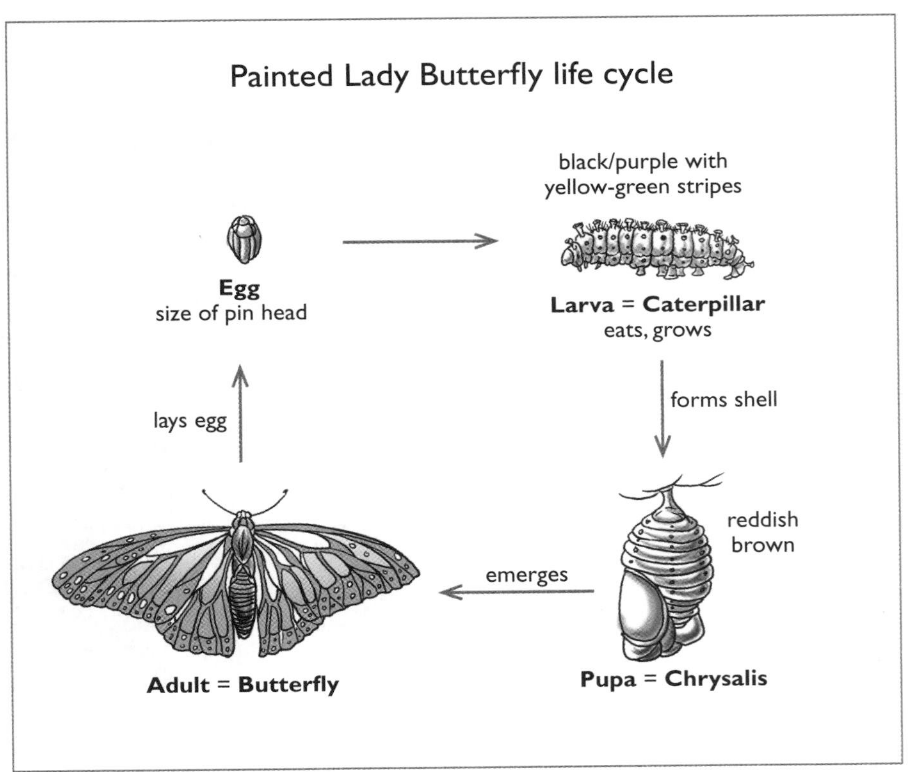

TEST 2 SPEAKING

Re-tell lecture

TIP STRIP

Scan the picture quickly to prepare for the lecture. As you listen, try to get an overall feeling for the meaning and the speaker's attitude.

Take notes but don't try to write every word you hear. Only write key words, e.g. *purpose of museums – relevant in info age? should be educ. – think about visitors, engage – social change, relevant.*

Think about how you will organize what you will say to be ready when the microphone opens.

In the test, there are 3–4 tasks. For each task, you see an image on the screen. Listen to the lecture and then speak into the microphone. The wording in the instructions below is the same as you will see in the actual test. See page 20 for help.

40 sec You will hear a lecture. After listening to the lecture, in 10 seconds, please speak into the microphone and retell what you have just heard from the lecture in your own words. You will have 40 seconds to give your response.

1 ▶ 52

2 ▶ 53

3 ▶ 54

Answer short question

In the test, there are 10–12 tasks. For each task, you hear a question and speak your answer into the microphone. The wording in the instructions below is the same as you will see in the actual test. See page 22 for help.

TIP STRIP

Listen for key words, e.g. in Question 1: *organs*, *chest*, *breathe*. If you do not know one of the words, e.g. *organs*, try to answer based on what you know: *What do we use to breathe?* The word *organs* is plural, so we know the answer should be plural.

55–64 10 sec. You will hear a question. Please give a simple and short answer. Often just one or a few words is enough.

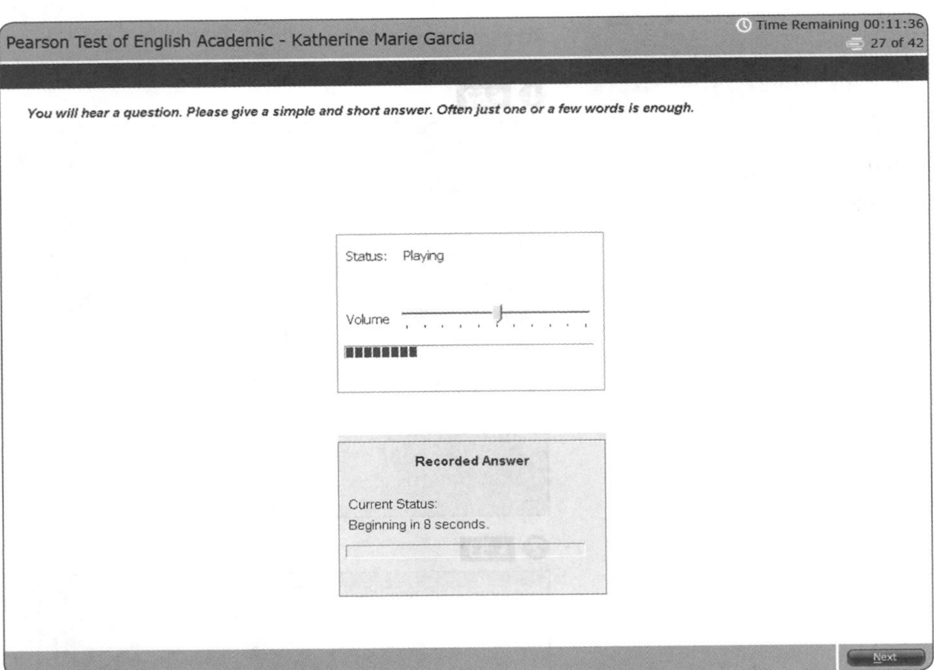

Answer short question: Each question is displayed on a new screen.

TEST 2

SPEAKING

Summarize written text

TIP STRIP

Read the passage for the overall meaning, then find the main idea of each paragraph. For example, in Passage 1 the first paragraph tells us how important sound is to most sea animals, the second paragraph is about the disturbance that noise made by boats causes to creatures underwater and the third paragraph qualifies the second by explaining that the effect of the man-made noises combine, and it is this build-up that causes problems. Shorten these ideas to put them into one sentence.

In the test, there are 2–3 tasks. Each task has a text on the screen. You type your summary of the text into the box at the bottom of the screen. The wording in the instructions below is the same as you will see in the actual test. See page 24 for help.

1  **10 min.** Read the passage below and summarize it using one sentence. Type your response in the box at the bottom of the screen. You have 10 minutes to finish this task. Your response will be judged on the quality of your writing and on how well your response presents the key points in the passage.

Most sea creatures, from whales and dolphins to fish, sharks, shrimps and possibly even anemones respond to sound, and many can produce it. They use it to hunt and to hide, find mates and food, form and guide shoals, navigate 'blind', send messages and transmit warnings, establish territories, warn off competitors, stun prey, deceive predators, and sense changes in water and conditions.

Marine animals click bones and grind teeth; use drum-tight bladders and special sonic organs to chirp, grunt, and boom; belch gases; and vibrate special organs. Far from the 'silent deep', the oceans are a raucous babel.

Into this age-long tumult, in the blink of an evolutionary eye, has entered a new thunder: the throb of mighty engines as 46,220 large vessels plough the world's shipping lanes. Scientists say that background noise in the ocean has increased roughly by 15 decibels in the past 50 years. It may not sound like much in overall terms; but it is enough, according to many marine biologists, to mask the normal sounds of ocean life going about its business. At its most intense, some even say noise causes whales to become disoriented, dolphins to develop 'the bends', fish to go deaf, flee their breeding grounds or fail to form shoals – enough to disrupt the basic biology of two thirds of the planet.

'Undersea noise pollution is like the death of a thousand cuts', says Sylvia Earle, chief scientist of the U.S. National Oceanic and Atmospheric Administration. 'Each sound in itself may not be a matter of critical concern, but taken all together, the noise from shipping, seismic surveys, and military activity is creating a totally different environment than existed even 50 years ago. That high level of noise is bound to have a hard, sweeping impact on life in the sea.'

....

....

....

....

....

TEST 2

WRITING

2 10 min Read the passage below and summarize it using one sentence. Type your response in the box at the bottom of the screen. You have 10 minutes to finish this task. Your response will be judged on the quality of your writing and on how well your response presents the key points in the passage.

Humans have been cultivating chillies as food for 6,000 years, but we are still learning new things about the science behind their heat and how it reacts with our body. In the late 1990s, scientists identified the pain nerves that detect capsaicin: the chemical in chillies responsible for most of the burning sensation in our mouth. But it's only during the last few years that scientists have also learnt why chillies evolved to be spicy in the first place, and they have managed to cultivate new varieties that are up to 300 times hotter than the common Jalapeno.

The hottest part of a chilli is not the seeds, as many people think, but the white flesh that houses the seeds, known as the placenta. But why did chillies evolve to be hot in the first place? Most scientists believe capsaicin acts mainly as a deterrent against would-be mammal predators such as rodents. But recent research suggests this may not be the whole story. US scientists working in Bolivia have studied how hot and mild chillies differ in their susceptibility to a certain harmful fungus. It turns out that the hotter the chilli, the better its defences against the fungus, leading the researchers to propose that heat may have evolved to help chillies deal with harmful microbes, as well as hungry mammals.

....

....

....

....

....

Write essay

TIP STRIP

Identify the key words in the statement and note them on your Erasable Noteboard Booklet. For example, in Question 1: *school – students stay to 18?*

Decide what your opinion is going to be. You do not have to agree or disagree completely but you need to be clear on your position and why you believe it. Make some brief notes for your argument before you start to write.

In the test, there are 1–2 tasks. For each task, the essay question is on the screen. You type your essay into the box on the screen. The wording in the instructions below is the same as you will see in the actual test. See page 27 for help.

20 min. **You will have 20 minutes to plan, write and revise an essay about the topic below. Your response will be judged on how well you develop a position, organize your ideas, present supporting details, and control the elements of standard written English. You should write 200–300 words.**

1. 'Students should be required to stay in school until the age of eighteen.'
   To what extent do you agree or disagree with this statement? Support your point of view with reasons and/or examples from your own experience.

2. 'Environmental problems are too great to be managed by individuals so real change can only be achieved at government level.'
   To what extent do you agree or disagree with this statement? Support your point of view with reasons and/or examples from your own experience.

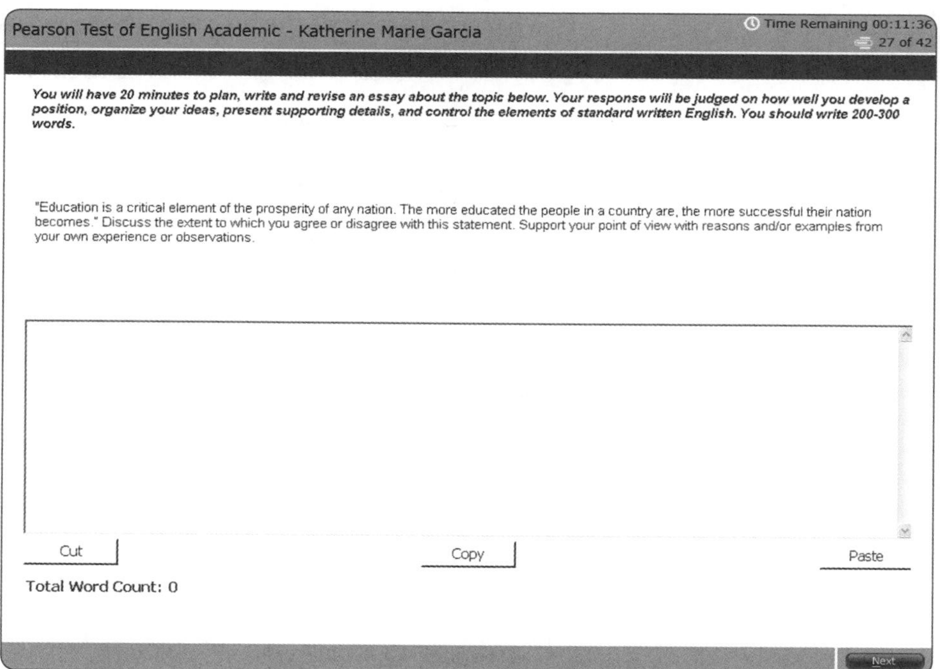

Write essay: Each question is displayed on a new screen.

Multiple-choice, choose single answer

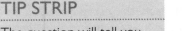

TIP STRIP

The question will tell you what information to look for. In Question 1, you must find a problem in relation to sea snails. Note that the first sentence of the passage refers to *dangers of sea snails*, so you know the problem is one caused by sea snails.

In the test, there are 2–3 tasks. For each task, you read the text on the left of the screen and look at the options on the right of the screen. You click the button next to the answer you think is correct. The wording in the instructions below is the same as you will see in the actual test. See page 30 for help.

Read the text and answer the multiple-choice question by selecting the correct response. ***Only one response is correct.***

1 Submarine operators have been alerted to the dangers of sea snails in a recent study. An international research team says the hardy deep-sea animals latch on to the submarines used by scientists, potentially spreading disease in pristine ecosystems.

The limpet is a sea snail that lives 2,000 metres underwater but can also survive in air when a submarine emerges from the water. If it goes unnoticed, the limpet can find itself in another habitat the next time the submarine is used. As 90 per cent of limpets are infected by parasites, this poses a threat to the ecosystem; but thoroughly cleaning the submarines will solve the problem.

What problem does the article mention in relation to sea snails?

- ○ A Research into sea snails has been harming the animals themselves.
- ○ B Sea snails are being carried by submarines to places where they harm other species.
- ○ C Sea snails are spreading diseases to the research scientists on submarines.
- ○ D Dirty submarines are endangering the well-being of the sea snails that attach themselves.

2 The Graphic Design degree provides students with a nurturing environment for learning, developing aesthetic appreciation and design skills with an emphasis on media and marketing. Students have the chance to develop their personal style, while broadening their technical repertoire as designers.

The academic staff are former working artists, theorists and designers who have been successful in achieving major awards, commissions and research grants. The facilities for the graphic design program include spacious design studios, colour and monochrome darkrooms and photography studios. Students will develop skills at a professional working standard in all computer-based programs that the design industry requires.

What does the Graphic Design degree offer students?

- ○ A experience working on new magazines
- ○ B the opportunity to apply for funds to help with their study
- ○ C teachers who have practical experience in a creative field
- ○ D the use of state-of-the-art cameras

Multiple-choice, choose multiple answers

TIP STRIP

Words in the options may not be exactly the same as the ones in the text. Remember, you do not need to know all these words; you will usually be able to guess the meaning if you know some of them. For example, in Text 1, if you know what a *canoe* is, you can guess that *rigging*, *sails* and *lengthy anchor warps* are equipment for boats.

In the test, there are 2–3 tasks. For each task, you read the text on the left of the screen and look at the options on the right of the screen. You click the buttons next to all of the answers you think are correct. The wording in the instructions below is the same as you will see in the actual test. See page 32 for help.

1 **Read the text and answer the question by selecting all the correct responses.** ***You will need to select more than one response.***

When the Maori people first came to New Zealand, they brought the mulberry plant from which they made bark cloth. However, the mulberry did not flourish in the new climate so they found a substitute in the native flax. They used this for baskets, mats, and fishing nets and to make intricate fibre ceremonial cloaks. Maori identified almost 60 types of flax, and propagated flax nurseries and plantations to supply the integral material. They chopped the leaves near the base of the flax plant using a sharp mussel shell or shaped rocks. The flesh of the leaf was stripped off right down to the fibre which went through several processes of washing, bleaching, softening, dyeing and drying. Flax ropes and cords had such great strength that they were used to bind together sections of hollowed-out logs to create huge ocean-going canoes, and to provide rigging, sails and lengthy anchor warps for them. It was also used for roofs for housing. The ends of the flax leaves were fanned out to make torches to provide light at night.

For which of the following purposes does the passage say the Maori used flax?

- ○ A special clothing
- ○ B cleaning cloth
- ○ C equipment for boats
- ○ D walls for their huts
- ○ E cooking tools

TEST 2

READING

❷ **Read the text and answer the question by selecting all the correct responses.** ***You will need to select more than one response.***

The Neue National Gallery in Berlin was designed by Mies van der Rohe. Built in 1968, it is a jump from the traditional museum concept of a closed building with exhibition rooms. Instead it is an open-plan, flexible space. With only two steel columns on each side, the corners are 'free', giving the building a lightweight look.

The gallery was the first building completed as part of a cluster of buildings dedicated to culture and the fine arts. It is often said that the building is a work of art in itself. The unusual natural illumination in the building, coming from around and below the viewer rather than above, has the effect of shocking the viewer out of their usual way of seeing and encouraging visitors to bring a fresh eye to the art.

The upper level is mainly used for special exhibits, for example, large-scale sculptures or paintings. The vast lower level has space for themed shows, and contains shops, a café, and the museum's permanent collection, which ranges from early modern art to art of the 1960s. The podium roof plaza is an open air gallery for public sculpture.

On request, guests may enter the garden to see figurative and abstract sculptures on display there. Special exhibits are attended by specially trained, very personable staff, who field questions, explain the exhibits, and enthuse about their favourite works.

What does the passage say can be found at the Neue National Gallery?

- ○ A overhead lighting to showcase artwork
- ○ B substantial pillars in the corners of the building
- ○ C artwork on top of the building
- ○ D several separate gallery rooms on each floor
- ○ E helpful guides to give information about the art

Re-order paragraphs

TIP STRIP

Reference words, e.g. *the*, *this* refer to something that has been mentioned before. Use this to help you order the text.

In Question 1, Sentence D introduces the idea of a conference; Sentence B refers to *the conference*, so it must come after the first mention in Sentence D.

Look at the reference to *this assistance* in Sentence C; it follows on from *to assist* in Sentence B and introduces the idea of industry professionals.

Sentence A follows this by mentioning *the industry professionals*.

In the test, there are 2–3 tasks. For each task, you drag paragraphs from the left and drop them into the correct order on the right. The wording in the instructions below is the same as you will see in the actual test. See page 35 for help.

The text boxes in the left panel have been placed in a random order. Restore the original order by dragging the text boxes from the left panel to the right panel.

1

A It is important to register for sessions with the industry professionals as numbers are limited.

B The conference is part of the career counselling centre's campaign, which has been designed to assist final year students transitioning out of university and getting their careers off to a good start.

C Students will be able to speak with industry professionals and graduates who had the benefit of this assistance last year.

D The University will host its second annual Arts and Commerce Career Readiness Conference on campus next month.

2

A Urban planners must consider these threats and work to allay them.

B Historically, in Europe and many other parts of the world, settlements were built on higher ground for the purposes of defence and to be close to fresh water sources.

C If the dangers are only in specific areas then they can make the affected regions into parkland or a green belt, often providing the added advantage of open space.

D Cities have often spread down from these locations onto coastal plains, putting them at risk of floods and storm surges.

Reading: Fill in the blanks

TIP STRIP

Read the text for overall meaning, e.g. Text 1 is about giving graduation gifts. Then look for clues in words like *despite*, which suggests an opposite idea to the positive idea of prosperity in *giving graduation gifts*, and *while*, which suggests another opposite idea: What do families have to be when choosing a gift if they do not have as much money? For the final gap, which word collocates with *lump*?

In the test, there are 4–5 tasks. For each task, you drag the words at the bottom of the text and drop them into the correct space in the text. The wording in the instructions below is the same as you will see in the actual test. See page 37 for help.

In the text below some words are missing. Drag words from the box below to the appropriate place in the text. To undo an answer choice, drag the word back to the box below the text.

1 The practice of giving graduation gifts seems to be alive and well, despite [1] ______ economic times. A recent study in the US has shown that while families may not have as much to spend, they are being more [2] ______ in the gifts they bestow. Lavish celebrations and large lump [3] ______ seem to have gone by the wayside in favour of smaller, more thoughtful gifts.

generous | hard | creative | money | sums | favourable

2 The majority of early pictures in the National Portrait Gallery's [1] ______ are by unknown artists, with fundamental questions, such as when, where and why they were painted still remaining to be answered. Through the application of scientific methods, a new project has the [2] ______ to unlock evidence that will allow researchers to determine answers to these questions. They will use a [3] ______ of cutting-edge scientific techniques, such as X-ray and infra-red reflectography, in order to reveal new [4] ______ about individual paintings.

information | potential | combination | prospect | connection | care | work

TEST 2 READING

In the text below some words are missing. Drag words from the box below to the appropriate place in the text. To undo an answer choice, drag the word back to the box below the text.

3 Gunpowder, also referred to as 'black powder', was the only [1] _____ chemical explosive until the mid-nineteenth century. It [2] _____ potassium nitrate, or 'saltpeter', which is an oxidiser, and a combination of charcoal and sulphur serves as fuel. There is [3] _____ consensus that gunpowder was initially invented in China as early as the ninth century. This [4] _____ to its use in fireworks and in gunpowder weapons.

includes | contains | caused | academic | known | unique | led

4 Marion Dorset (1872–1935) was an influential American biochemist. He began working as a [1] _____ for the U.S. Department of Agriculture in 1894, and worked his way up to become chief of the biochemical [2] _____ in 1904. He made important discoveries in bacterial toxins and animal diseases, and he conducted pioneering work in the [3] _____ of meat products. He co-discovered the virus that causes hog cholera and subsequently developed a [4] _____ to prevent it.

researcher | leader | serum | fluid | inspection | consumption | division

Reading & writing: Fill in the blanks

In the test, there are 5–6 tasks. For each task, you have a text with several gaps. You select the correct answer for each gap from the drop-down list on the screen. The wording in the instructions below is the same as you will see in the actual test. See page 40 for help.

TIP STRIP

Think about the grammar and vocabulary as well as the meaning for each gap. Look at Text 1, Question 1: Which tense is used for an event that happened in the past and is finished? In Question 2, which verb collocates with *role*? For Question 3, which relative pronoun is used after a non-defining relative clause (after a comma)? For Question 4, which option emphasizes the number of different contributions the Professor made?

Below is a text with blanks. Click on each blank, a list of choices will appear. Select the appropriate choice for each blank.

1 Victoria University of Wellington has conferred an honorary degree on a distinguished astrophysicist in a recent graduation ceremony. Professor Warrick Couch [1] ______ the honorary degree of Doctor of Science for his remarkable contribution to our knowledge of galaxies and dark energy. Professor Couch is a distinguished astrophysicist who has [2] ______ a crucial role in the discovery that the Universe is expanding at an accelerating rate, a finding which led to the lead scientists being awarded a Nobel Prize in Physics in 2011, which he attended in recognition of his contribution.

In his research, Professor Couch uses large ground-based and spaced-based telescopes to observe galaxy clusters, [3] ______ are the largest structures in the Universe. He is also involved in a number of national and international committees overseeing the management of these telescopes. [4] ______ his own research activities, Professor Couch has worked to support young researchers and provide public comment on astronomy internationally.

1	A was receiving	B had received	C is received	D received
2	A played	B found	C done	D led
3	A those	B which	C they	D who
4	A In addition to	B As a result of	C Regarding	D Instead of

2 Keith Haring began as an underground artist, literally. His first famous projects were pieces of stylized graffiti [1] ______ in New York subway stations. Haring travelled from station to station, drawing with chalk and chatting with commuters about his work. These doodles helped him develop his classic style and he grew so [2] ______, doing up to 40 drawings a day, that it was not long before fame and a measure of fortune followed.

Soon, galleries and collectors from the art establishment wanted to buy full-sized pieces by Haring. The paintings skyrocketed in price but this did not sit well with Haring's philosophy. He believed that art, or [3] ______ his art, was for everyone. Soon, Haring opened a store which he called the Pop Shop, which he hoped would attract a broad range of people. While somewhat controversial among street artists, some of [4] ______ accused Haring of 'selling out', the Pop Shop changed the way people thought about the relationship between art and business.

1	A drawers	B drawn	C drew	D draws
2	A perceptive	B proactive	C pedantic	D prolific
3	A by contrast	B at least	C actually	D in part
4	A whose	B those	C whom	D them

Below is a text with blanks. Click on each blank, a list of choices will appear. Select the appropriate answer for each blank.

3 Conservationists have long debated whether the koala should go on the Australian national threatened species list. [1] ______ the koala is clearly in trouble in some parts of the country – in Queensland, for example, high numbers are afflicted by disease – in other parts such as Victoria and South Australia the problem is not that koala populations [2] ______ , but that they have grown to the point where they are almost too numerous.

For a species to be classed as vulnerable, its population [3] ______ by more than 30 percent over the last three generations or 10 years. The problem is that when such a stipulation is applied to koalas, the Victorian boom offsets the Queensland bust, and the species stays off the list.

This has repercussions because northern koalas are different to southern ones. They are smaller, for example, and they contain a genetic variation not represented in the South. [4] ______ , a split listing has been devised koalas from New South Wales, the ACT and Queensland are now officially 'Vulnerable'; those from Victoria and South Australia are not considered threatened.

1	A Because	B However	C Despite	D While
2	A had been falling	B were falling	C are falling	D had fallen
3	A must have decreased	B will be decreasing	C was decreased	D has decreased
4	A According to this	B For this reason	C For instance	D In contrast

4 The Department of Fine Arts is a vibrant department comprising active art professionals housed in a modern, well-equipped facility. The faculty enjoys [1] ______ relationships with local museums, numerous galleries and a variety of other art organizations. Fine Arts students benefit from studying with artistically [2] ______ mentors who exhibit and research regionally, nationally and internationally. The department provides students with many opportunities for artistic and personal [3] ______ through daily contact with full-time faculty members who are noted artists and researchers. Classes are small to allow for personalised feedback and guidance.

Well-appointed studios on campus [4] ______ the daily practice of art in combination with the study of liberal arts. During their studies, students gain exposure to world-class visiting artists and exhibitions, and also have local and international travel [5] ______ .

1	A corresponding	B collaborative	C combined	D common
2	A activating	B actively	C activity	D active
3	A growing	B growth	C grown	D grow
4	A facilitating	B facilities	C facilitate	D facility
5	A contingencies	B opportunities	C occasions	D needs

Below is a text with blanks. Click on each blank, a list of choices will appear. Select the appropriate answer for each blank.

5 Lyrebirds, a common bird in rainforest areas of Australia, have an incredible repertoire of sounds that they are able to mimic from their environment, including over 20 other bird calls as well as sophisticated mechanical sounds. They [1] ______ to replicate the sounds of chainsaws and pneumatic drills. The male lyrebird sings a medley of mimicry to impress females – and the more detailed and varied his repertoire is, the more interesting it seems to potential [2] ______. Like females of other bird species, female lyrebirds do not [3] ______ in the imitating, but simply judge the competing males' symphonies. Once learned, it seems a lyrebird rarely forgets a call, and the sounds are passed down through the generations. There are some lyrebirds in Victoria, Australia, that [4] ______ recreate the sounds of axes, saws and old-fashioned cameras which have not been used in the area for years.

1	A have been known	B are being known	C are knowing	D know
2	A companions	B spouses	C mates	D pairs
3	A put forward	B take place	C work out	D take part
4	A indeed	B still	C just	D yet

TEST 2

READING

Summarize spoken text

TIP STRIP

The first part of the lecture usually introduces the topic, e.g. in Question 1: proofreading. Listen for the main ideas and take notes of key words only, using abbreviations, e.g. in Question 1: *proofreading – hard to see own grammar, punct errors – eliminate past errors – look for logical org – paras – read aloud – check refs – have break before proofreading.*

In the test, there are 2–3 tasks. For each task, you listen to the audio then type your summary into the box on the screen. The wording in the instructions below is the same as you will see in the actual test. See page 45 for help.

You will hear a short lecture. Write a summary for a fellow student who was not present at the lecture. You should write 50–70 words.

10 min. You will have 10 minutes to finish this task. Your response will be judged on the quality of your writing and on how well your response presents the key points presented in the lecture.

1 ▸ 65

....

....

....

....

....

....

2 ▸ 66

....

....

....

....

....

....

Multiple-choice, choose multiple answers

In the test, there are 2–3 tasks. For each task, you listen to the audio then click the buttons next to all of the answers you think are correct. The wording in the instructions below is the same as you will see in the actual test. See page 47 for help.

TIP STRIP

Read the question before the audio begins to know what to listen for. In Question 1, you are listening for comments about students.

As you listen, eliminate or confirm options, e.g. when you hear: *We've built a reputation for producing both traditional and alternative performances*, which option can be eliminated? When the speaker says: … *for the level of support that's available, and I mean from the tutors as well as from fellow students and alumni*, which option can be confirmed?

Listen to the recording and answer the question by selecting all the correct responses. ***You will need to select more than one response.***

1 ▸ 67 **What comments are made about students in the Theatre Studies program?**

- ○ A They are encouraged to focus their studies on modern productions.
- ○ B Past students offer them help.
- ○ C Students can work at their own pace.
- ○ D They need to be clear from the start about the area they want to work in.
- ○ E A high percentage complete the degree and get jobs in their field.

2 ▸ 68 **What was significant about the rock art found in the Yunnan province and in Western Europe?**

- ○ A The skill in the rock art is superior to that found in other parts of the world.
- ○ B It suggests that the ancestors of the rock artists may have once lived in the same area.
- ○ C Rock art in both places depicted animals of interest to humans.
- ○ D It showed the people in each place had very different lifestyles.
- ○ E It shows that people in widely separated places thought the same way.

Fill in the blanks

TIP STRIP

Skim the text briefly to get an idea what it is about, e.g. in Question 1, it is about barred owls.

Use the few seconds before the recording starts to look carefully at the gaps and the words preceding each one, so that you do not miss your cue to write the word.

As you write, make sure that the word makes sense in the context, e.g. in Question 1, Gap 1 *small* [ ] suggests that the next word will be a noun.

In the test, there are 2–3 tasks. For each task, there is a text with several gaps. You type the correct answer for each gap into the box in the text. The wording in the instructions below is the same as you will see in the actual test. See page 49 for help.

You will hear a recording. Type the missing words in each blank.

1 ▶ 69

Barred owls can be found in dense forests right across North America. They feed on small [1] [ ], fish, birds and small reptiles – pretty much anything that comes their way. The barred owl grows up to half a metre tall and has emerged as a very [2] [ ] nocturnal predator. Whereas they have been long-thought to live in old-growth forests, they are now building up quite an [3] [ ] population. In Charlotte, North Carolina, barred owls tend to nest in the cavities of the numerous willow oak trees that line the city's streets. Far from being endangered, the owls have expanded their range; and now, in some places, conservationists are worried about the effects they might have on other [4] [ ] species.

2 ▶ 70

Before the beginning of the 1900s, the only way to obtain pearls was by collecting very large numbers of pearl oysters from the ocean floor by hand. The oysters – or sometimes mussels – were brought to the surface, opened, and [1] [ ]. More than a ton of these had to be checked in order to find just three or four quality pearls. Divers often descended to depths of over 100 feet on just one single breath. Now, of course this exposed them to [2] [ ] creatures and dangerous waves, not to mention drowning. In some areas, divers put grease on their bodies to conserve heat and they held a large [3] [ ], like a rock, to descend so they didn't have to exert effort going down. Today, pearl diving has pretty much been supplanted by cultured pearl [4] [ ]. Particles are implanted in the oyster to encourage the formation of pearls, and this allows for more predictable production. The divers who still work, do so mainly for the [5] [ ] industry.

Highlight correct summary

TIP STRIP

Take notes as you listen; just key words and ideas. In Question 1, these could be: *advantages of telecommuting; things companies should consider; employee suitability to work away from office.*

Read through the summaries and eliminate any that contain information that is wrong or that you did not hear in the passage. Then eliminate any summaries that focus on only part of the message or do not cover the main points.

In the test, there are 2–3 tasks. For each task, you listen to the audio then click the button next to the summary you think is correct. The wording in the instructions below is the same as you will see in the actual test. See page 51 for help.

You will hear a recording. Click on the paragraph that best relates to the recording.

1 ▶ 71

○ A Company leaders have to be careful that they do not have one set of practices for those in the office and another for those who telecommute. Besides needing to be fair at all times, managers will find that a telecommuting arrangement will simply not work if workers feel isolated and excluded from the company culture.

○ B Telecommuting has a lot of advantages but to make it work, company leaders need to plan in advance to ensure that they anticipate issues for example training, security and communication. They also need to ensure that they hire workers who are suited to working remotely and ensure equal access to resources and advancement.

○ C When workers ask if they can work from home, companies should consider a telecommuting arrangement, as it has several advantages for businesses as well as workers. There is money to be saved on overheads and training but for telecommuting to function properly, only independent staff should be allowed to work in this way.

○ D Managers should not rush into letting their employees telecommute. It may sound good because businesses can save money on things like office space, but if workers' needs and ambitions are not well catered for in the arrangement, the company culture will ultimately be damaged and they may even be sued.

You will hear a recording. Click on the paragraph that best relates to the recording.

❷ ▸ 72

- ○ A While many of us believe that we enjoy making choices, several studies have shown that this is not in fact the case. When faced with choosing from several types of jam, consumers were interested at first but soon became overloaded with choice. They simply abandoned the choice and went back to their favourite brands.
- ○ B The incredible range of choices that consumers now have is making business difficult for companies who have to provide more and more choices to keep up with the market but also for consumers who expect choice but give up without making any choices at all if they feel confused by the wide range on offer.
- ○ C Consumers face more choices than they did in the past and a study showed shoppers are attracted if a number of options are presented to them. However, those options still need to be of a good quality and something that appeals to the consumer or, as in the study, they will walk away without making a purchase.
- ○ D With a wide range of choices, one would expect consumers to buy more products. However, a consumer experiment found that when customers had many choices, they were likely to sample the products but became overwhelmed and did not buy much, whereas they were more likely to buy something when they had far fewer options to choose from.

Multiple-choice, choose single answer

TIP STRIP

Read the questions and options quickly before the recording begins.

In Question 1, you know you will hear statements about something called the 'Beehive' (option 1), which is a building (option 2) in New Zealand (option 3) that people may have disliked once (option 4).

As you listen, try to eliminate or confirm the options.

In the test, there are 2–3 tasks. For each task, you listen to the audio then click the button next to the answer you think is correct. The wording in the instructions below is the same as you will see in the actual test. See page 54 for help.

Listen to the recording and answer the multiple-choice question by selecting the correct response. *Only one response is correct.*

1 ▶ 73 What does the speaker say about the 'Beehive'?

- ○ A Its name comes from being a centre of activity.
- ○ B Its architect saw the project through to completion.
- ○ C It used to be a symbol of national pride for New Zealand.
- ○ D It has come back into favour in recent years.

2 ▶ 74 What does the speaker say can be done to avoid conflict within study groups?

- ○ A Group members should have compatible personalities.
- ○ B Tasks should be approached in a creative way.
- ○ C The main task should be divided into parts.
- ○ D Long-range goals need to be given priority.

TEST 2 LISTENING

Select missing word

TIP STRIP

Use the instructions to orient yourself to the topic, e.g. in Question 1, the topic is *studying humanities*.

As you listen, notice the direction of the speaker's argument, so that you can anticipate what ideas are coming, e.g. in Question 1, the speaker is arguing a point of view, so the missing words will be part of that argument.

In the test, there are 2–3 tasks. For each task, you listen to the audio then click the button next to the words you think complete the audio. The wording in the instructions below is the same as you will see in the actual test. See page 56 for help.

1 ▶ 75 You will hear a recording about studying humanities. *At the end of the recording the last word or group of words has been replaced by a beep.* Select the correct option to complete the recording.

○ A from a number of angles

○ B with a specific goal in mind

○ C in a less emotional manner

○ D in a way that enriches society

2 ▶ 76 You will hear a recording about surfing. *At the end of the recording the last word or group of words has been replaced by a beep.* Select the correct option to complete the recording.

○ A could fail

○ B took place

○ C were at stake

○ D were discovered

Highlight incorrect words

TEST 2 LISTENING

TIP STRIP

Skim the transcription briefly to give you a general idea of the passage, and as you listen, read each word carefully. Often, the word you read and the word you hear will be very similar. There is a word like this in the first sentence of Transcription 1.

In the test, there are 2–3 tasks. For each task, you listen to the audio and follow the words in the text on the screen. You click on the words that are different on the screen and the audio. The wording in the instructions below is the same as you will see in the actual test. See page 58 for help.

You will hear a recording. Below is a transcription of the recording. ***Some words in the transcription differ from what the speaker said.*** **Please click on the words that are different.**

1 ▶ 77 Transcription:

Well, there are many factors that can cause one species to diverge into two. One of these is when populations get isolated from each other by something like a lagoon forming or forest being cleared. And there's another idea that as individuals adapt to their environment, this might have a knock-on impact on mate choice, a process called sensitive drive speciation. Now this seems to occur in cichlid fish. They have shown that a female preference for either red or blue striped males only exists in clean water, where they are actually able to see.

2 ▶ 78 Transcription:

Social capital is a concept that was introduced by sociologists, many years ago. It's actually the networks and reserves that people use to deliver social outcomes. For instance, it might be holding a sporting event, running a community fair, being part of a club.

It is difficult to measure social capital and one way of looking at it is the amount that people volunteer in their local community. So you can consider the volunteering rate as an index for how healthy a community is. You can also look at something called a well-being index – the way people think about their lives and how accepting they are of others, their general perception of the value of their life.

Write from dictation

In the test, there are 3–4 tasks. For each task, you listen and type the sentence you hear into the box on the screen. The wording in the instructions below is the same as you will see in the actual test. See page 60 for help.

TIP STRIP

Write as much as you can, and continue writing so that you do not miss the rest of the sentence. Do not go back and correct words until the sentence has finished.

Before you click 'Next', check the grammar and spelling; and if you are unsure of the spelling, think of the rules of spelling.

You will hear a sentence. Type the sentence in the box below exactly as you hear it. Write as much of the sentence as you can. You will hear the sentence only once.

1 ▸ 79

....

....

....

2 ▸ 80

....

....

....

3 ▸ 81

....

....

....

TEST 3

Read aloud

In the test, there are 6–7 tasks. For each task, you read the text aloud into the microphone. The wording in the instructions below is the same as you will see in the actual test. See page 12 for help.

40 sec. Look at the text below. In 40 seconds, you must read this text aloud as naturally and as clearly as possible. You have 40 seconds to read aloud.

1. Tidal energy, also known as tidal power, is a renewable source of energy and a form of hydropower used to generate electricity from the energy of the tides. Though not currently widely utilised, due to high costs and limited availability, it can be called the energy resource of the future given the current rate of depletion of energy resources.

2. Certain types of methodology are more suitable for some research projects than others. For example, the use of questionnaires and surveys is more suitable for quantitative research whereas interviews and focus groups are more often used for qualitative research purposes.

3. Most countries are affected by labour migration. In many rural places, the traditional extended family has been undermined by the need for family members to migrate to towns as an economic necessity. Migration, therefore, presents a major challenge everywhere to social and economic policy.

4. One of the major factors influencing future home design will be the probable change in climate, with hotter summers, colder winters, and the possibility of floods. Consequently, houses will be built with better insulation and will also need ways of keeping cool in hot weather, whether that's air conditioning or more shading of windows.

5. Until fairly recent times, the origin of birds was one of evolution's great mysteries. This is no longer the case. Fossil evidence from China now conclusively proves that there is an evolutionary link between birds and several types of extinct prehistoric reptiles which lived millions of years ago, or in other words, dinosaurs.

6. Group work is valuable because of the opportunities it provides for students to develop collaboration and communication skills. As an assessment task, it has the potential to pose difficulties in relation to appropriate acknowledgement of authorship of individual group members. These difficulties can be minimised by ensuring that the task is well designed, with the roles of individuals effectively identified.

Repeat sentence

In the test, there are 10–12 tasks. For each task, you listen and repeat the sentence you hear into the microphone. The wording in the instructions below is the same as you will see in the actual test. See page 14 for help.

▸ 82–91 15 sec. You will hear a sentence. Please repeat the sentence exactly as you hear it. You will hear the sentence only once.

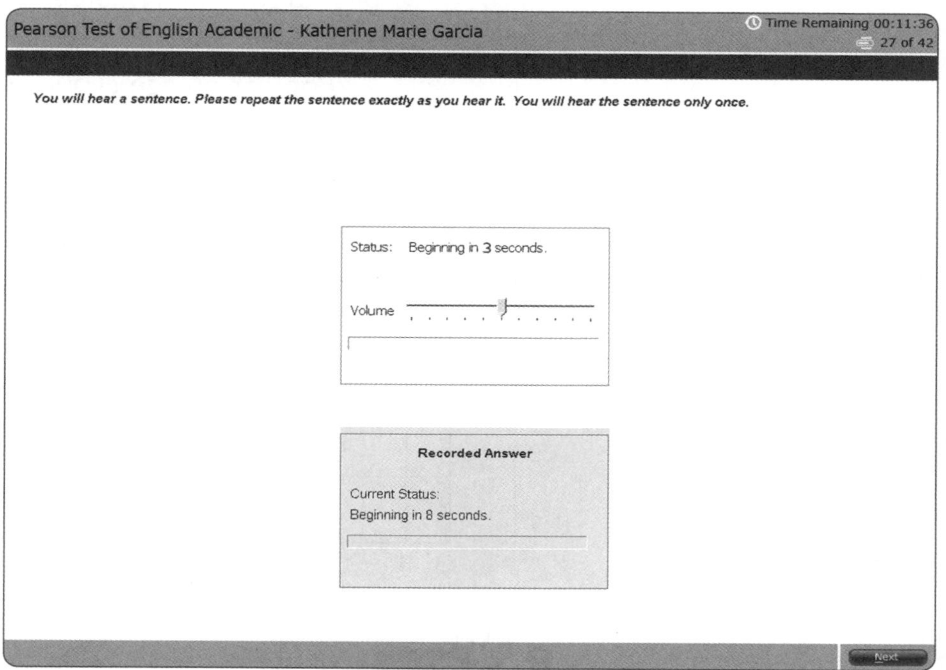

Repeat sentence: Each question is displayed on a new screen.

Describe image

In the test, there are 6–7 tasks. For each task, you look at the image and describe it into the microphone. The wording in the instructions below is the same as you will see in the actual test. See page 16 for help.

1 40 sec. Look at the chart below. In 25 seconds, please speak into the microphone and describe in detail what the chart is showing. You will have 40 seconds to give your response.

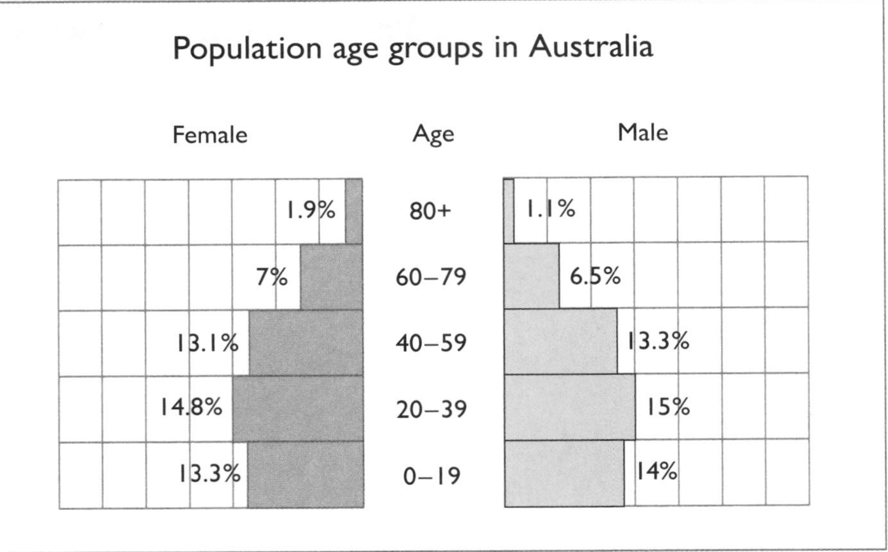

2 40 sec. Look at the diagram below. In 25 seconds, please speak into the microphone and describe in detail what the diagram is showing. You will have 40 seconds to give your response.

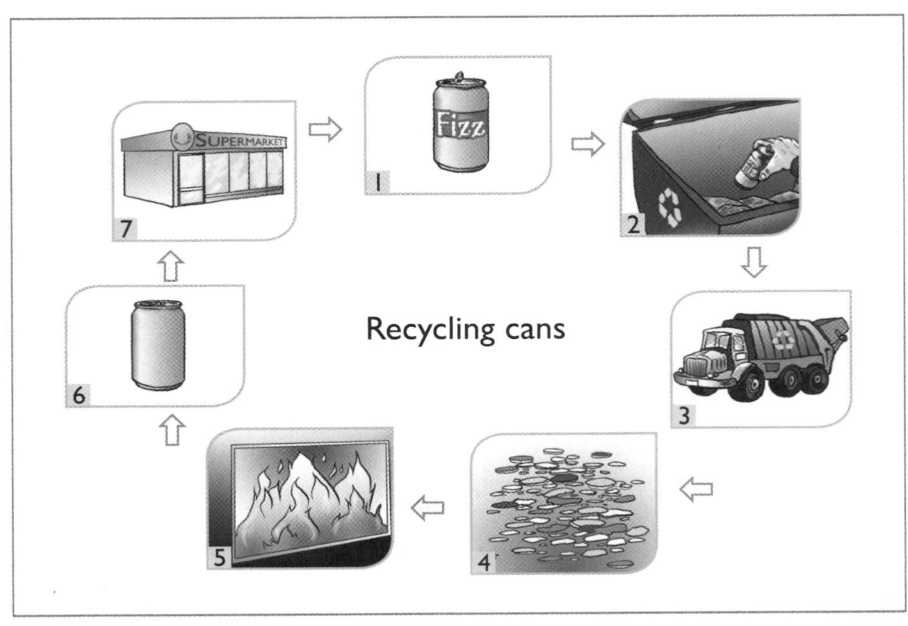

3 40 sec. Look at the chart below. In 25 seconds, please speak into the microphone and describe in detail what the chart is showing. You will have 40 seconds to give your response.

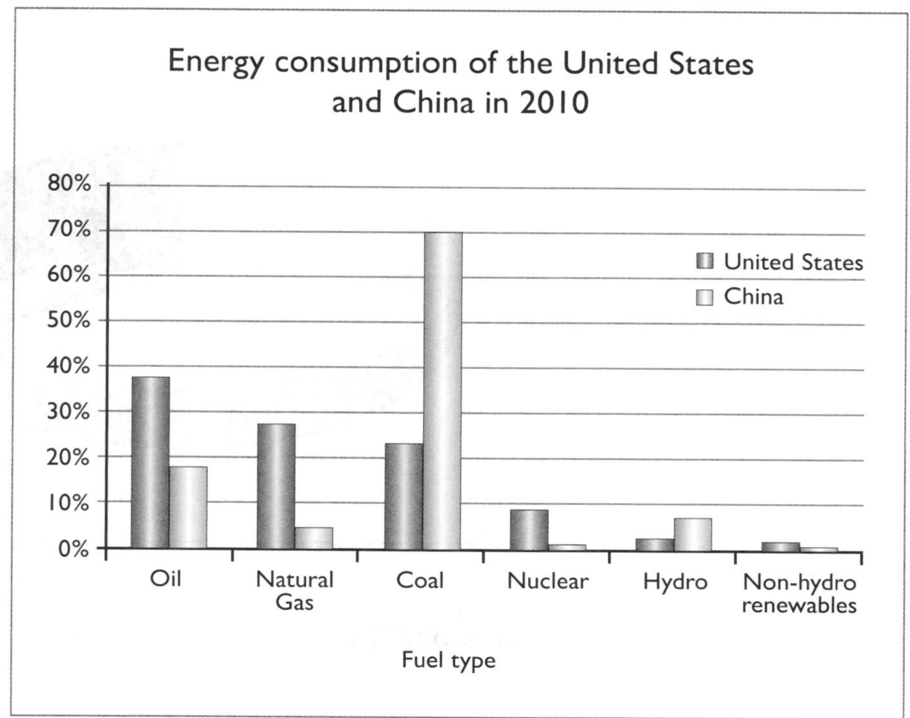

4 40 sec. Look at the diagram below. In 25 seconds, please speak into the microphone and describe in detail what the diagram is showing. You will have 40 seconds to give your response.

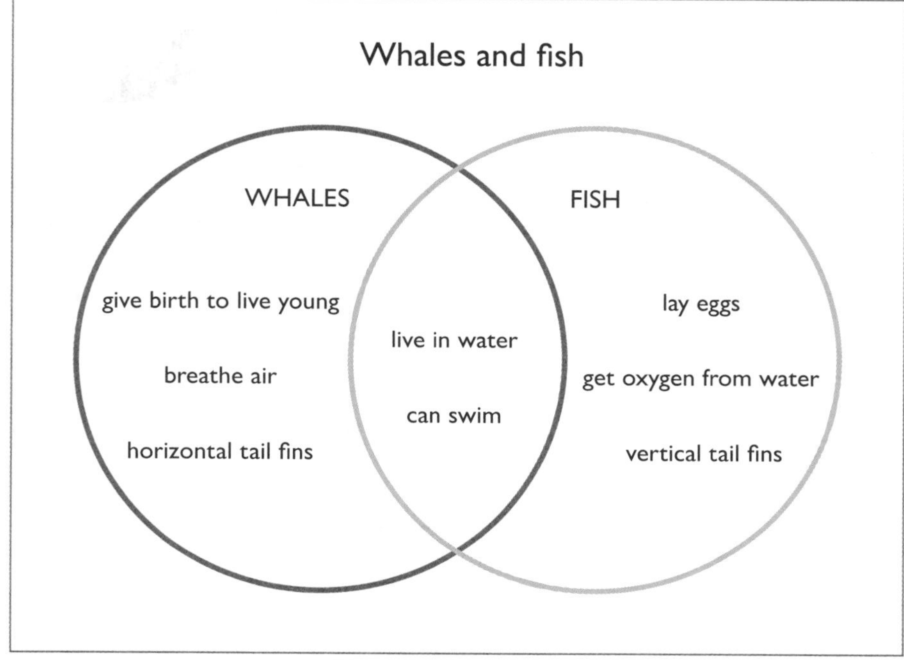

5 40 sec. Look at the chart below. In 25 seconds, please speak into the microphone and describe in detail what the chart is showing. You will have 40 seconds to give your response.

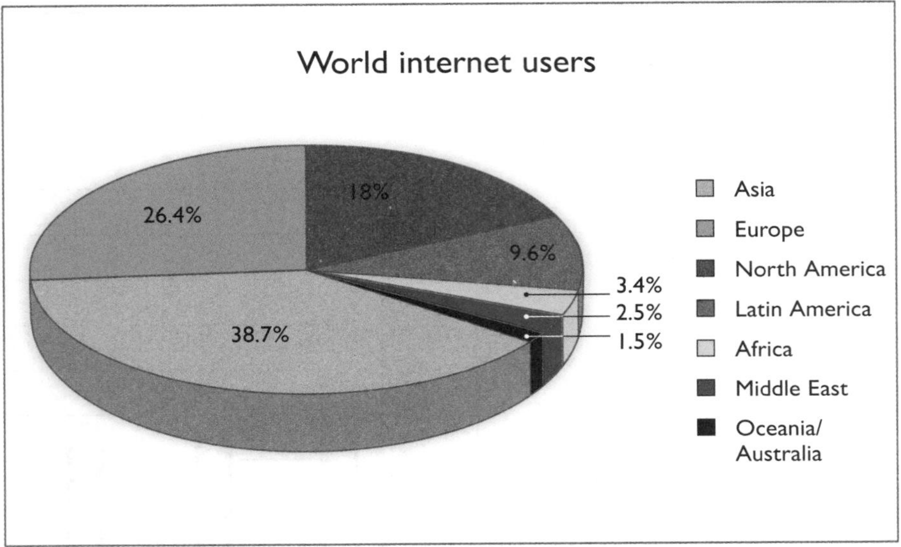

6 40 sec. Look at the diagram below. In 25 seconds, please speak into the microphone and describe in detail what the diagram is showing. You will have 40 seconds to give your response.

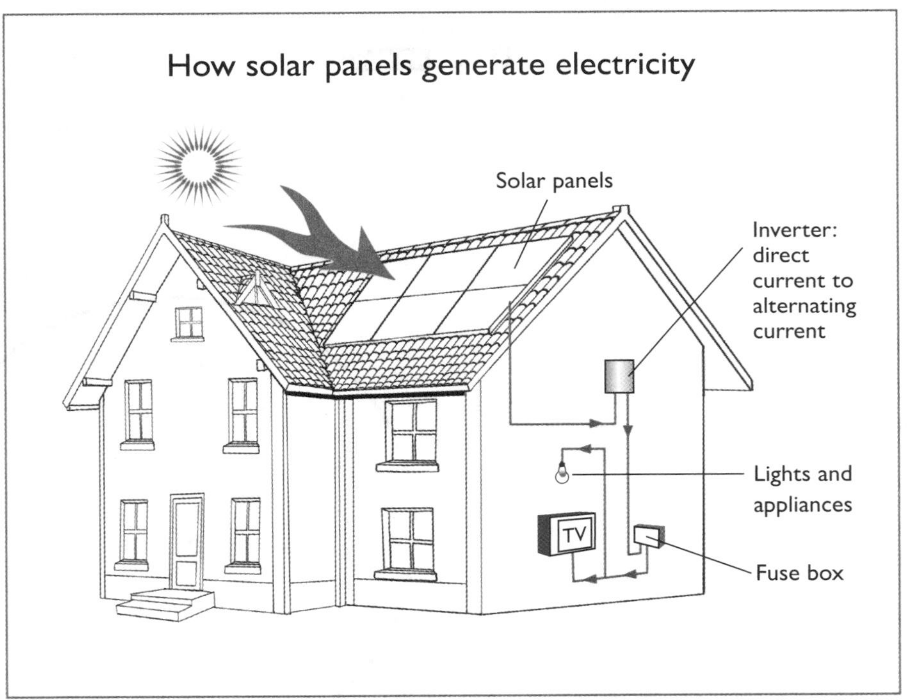

TEST 3 SPEAKING

Re-tell lecture

In the test, there are 3–4 tasks. For each task, you see an image on the screen. Listen to the lecture and then speak into the microphone. The wording in the instructions below is the same as you will see in the actual test. See page 20 for help.

40 sec. You will hear a lecture. After listening to the lecture, in 10 seconds, please speak into the microphone and retell what you have just heard from the lecture in your own words. You will have 40 seconds to give your response.

1 ▸ 92

2 ▸ 93

3 ▸ 94

Answer short question

In the test, there are 10–12 tasks. For each task, you hear a question and speak your answer into the microphone. The wording in the instructions below is the same as you will see in the actual test. See page 22 for help.

▸ 95–104  10 sec. You will hear a question. Please give a simple and short answer. Often just one or a few words is enough.

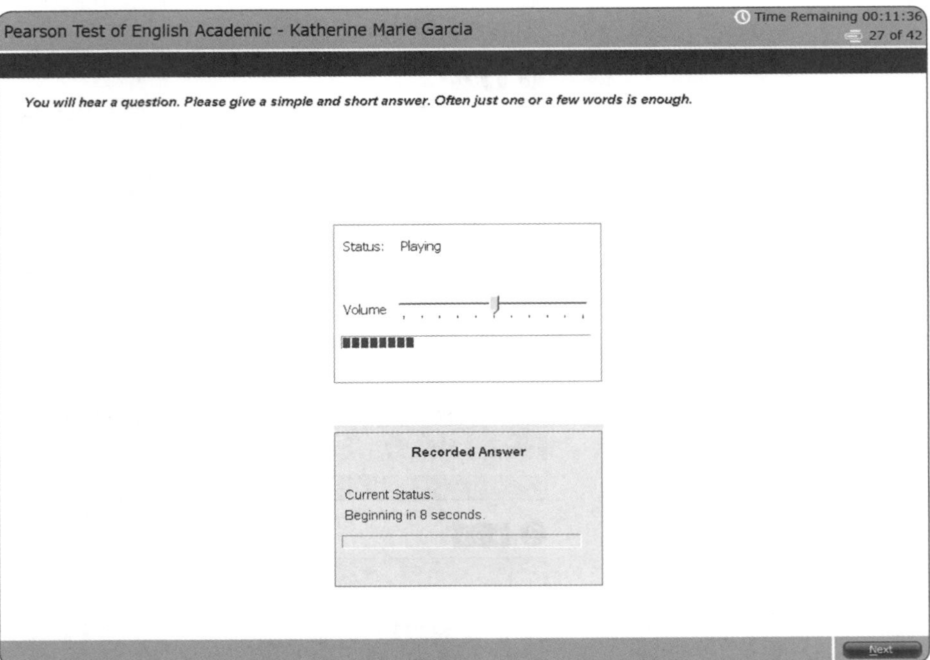

Answer short question: Each question is displayed on a new screen.

TEST 3
SPEAKING

Summarize written text

In the test, there are 2–3 tasks. Each task has a text on the screen. You type your summary of the text into the box at the bottom of the screen. The wording in the instructions below is the same as you will see in the actual test. See page 24 for help.

1 **10 min.** Read the passage below and summarize it using one sentence. Type your response in the box at the bottom of the screen. You have 10 minutes to finish this task. Your response will be judged on the quality of your writing and on how well your response presents the key points in the passage.

> Inequality between world citizens used to be determined in equal measures by class and location. New research, however, reveals that people's fortunes are being dictated primarily by where they live. As a result, economic migration has become the key way for individuals from developing countries to improve their economic standing, and governments will not be able to alleviate the pressure of migration on their societies until global inequality is reduced.
>
> In *Global Inequality: from class to location, from proletarians to migrants*, Branko Milanovic, of the University of Maryland, examines the differences in income between countries and concludes that a key priority for policy makers should be aid and support for developing countries.
>
> 'Not only is the overall inequality between world citizens greater in the early 21st century than it was more than a century and a half ago, but its composition has entirely changed; from being an inequality determined in equal measures by class and location, it has become preponderantly an inequality determined by location only,' finds the report. 'Analysis of incomes across countries for different members of the population reveals a wide gap between the underprivileged in wealthy societies and in less wealthy countries. This fact is of great political and economic significance. Individuals can now make large gains from migrating to wealthier countries.'

2 10 min. Read the passage below and summarize it using one sentence. Type your response in the box at the bottom of the screen. You have 10 minutes to finish this task. Your response will be judged on the quality of your writing and on how well your response presents the key points in the passage.

English is the world's lingua franca, the language of science, technology, business, diplomacy and popular culture. That probably explains why it is the world's most widely spoken language. It probably also explains why native English speakers are so reluctant to learn a second language. It's not worth the effort.

In 2005, the European Commission carried out a survey of the European Union's 25 member states. The two with the lowest rates of bilingualism – defined as being able to hold a conversation in more than one language – were the UK and Ireland. About two-thirds of people in these countries speak only English. It's a similar story wherever English is spoken as the mother tongue. Only about 25 per cent of US citizens can converse in another language. In Australia, the rates are even lower.

Compare that with continental Europe, where multilingualism is the rule rather than the exception. More than half of EU citizens are bilingual, and not just because they live in countries like Luxembourg with multiple official languages. Even in France, which has only one official language and is immensely proud of its linguistic heritage, most people speak a second language.

Again, that is largely down to the dominance of English. Across Europe, English is by far the most commonly learned language. High levels of bilingualism are not driven by a general desire to learn languages but a specific need to learn English.

....

....

....

....

....

Write essay

In the test, there are 1–2 tasks. For each task, the essay question is on the screen. You type your essay into the box on the screen. The wording in the instructions below is the same as you will see in the actual test. See page 27 for help.

20 min. You will have 20 minutes to plan, write and revise an essay about the topic below. Your response will be judged on how well you develop a position, organize your ideas, present supporting details, and control the elements of standard written English. You should write 200–300 words.

❶ 'Some types of employment are more suitable for men and other types of employment are more appropriate for women.'

To what extent do you agree with this statement? Support your point of view with reasons and examples from your own experience.

❷ 'Nowadays many young people leave home at an early age to either study or work in another city.'

Do you think this has more advantages or disadvantages for young people? Support your point of view with reasons and examples from your own experience.

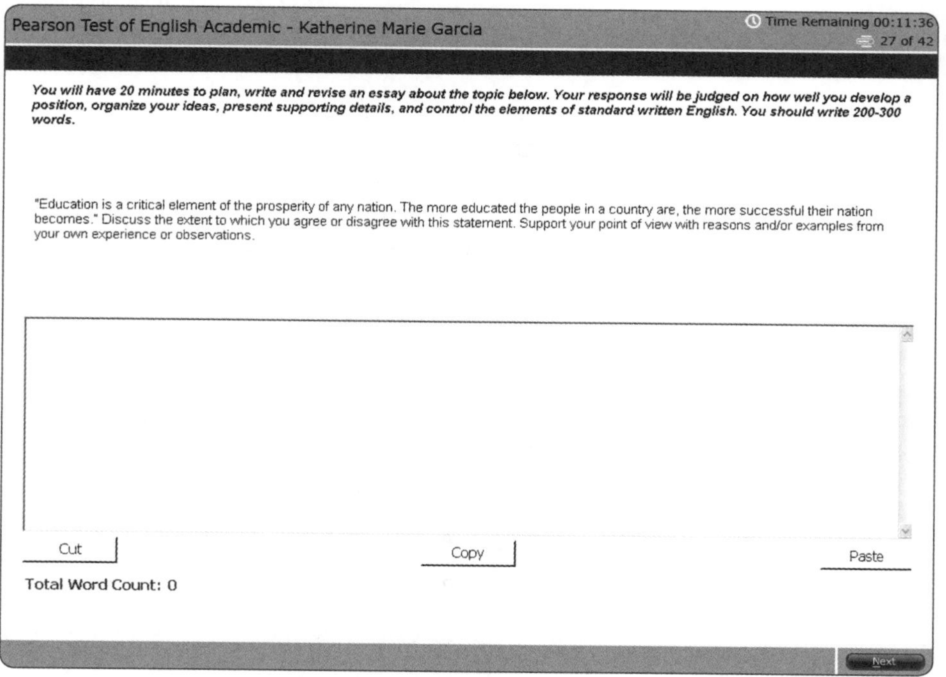

Write essay: Each question is displayed on a new screen.

Multiple-choice, choose single answer

In the test, there are 2–3 tasks. For each task, you read the text on the left of the screen and look at the options on the right of the screen. You click the button next to the answer you think is correct. The wording in the instructions below is the same as you will see in the actual test. See page 30 for help.

Read the text and answer the multiple-choice question by selecting the correct response. *Only one response is correct.*

1 Governments, business and many types of institutions collect, organise and record statistics. Statistics capture vital information about such things as the economy, population and the environment and therefore allow meaningful comparisons to be made. This can then inform decisions and plans made about such issues which in turn become public policies. While it may be the issues behind the statistics, rather than the statistics as such that command the public's attention, it must be recognised that it is the figures that inform these issues.

The author considers statistics to be important because

- ○ A they are recorded by official organisations.
- ○ B the general public have an interest in them.
- ○ C they are affected by plans and policies.
- ○ D they assist in driving public issues.

2 There are innumerable different species on the planet. Nobody really knows how many species there are, although many scientists have tried to estimate it. However, the complexity of trying to do this makes it impossible to establish a definitive number with any confidence. This is probably due to the fact that new species are continually appearing, while at the same time existing species evolve and some become extinct. In the past, the number of new species appearing exceeded the number of those dying out. Nowadays, however, due to human activity, this trend has reversed and as a result we are in danger of seriously disturbing our ecosystem.

Why is it difficult to establish the number of species globally?

- ○ A There are too many species to count them all.
- ○ B The number of species is constantly changing.
- ○ C Currently, more species are appearing than are becoming extinct.
- ○ D Human action has upset the balance of the natural environment.

Multiple-choice, choose multiple answers

In the test, there are 2–3 tasks. For each task, you read the text on the left of the screen and look at the options on the right of the screen. You click the buttons next to all of the answers you think are correct. The wording in the instructions below is the same as you will see in the actual test. See page 32 for help.

1 Read the text and answer the question by selecting all the correct responses. ***You will need to select more than one response.***

Snow is formed when temperatures are low and there is moisture – in the form of tiny ice crystals – in the atmosphere. When these tiny ice crystals collide they stick together in clouds to become snowflakes. If enough ice crystals stick together, they'll become heavy enough to fall to the ground.

Precipitation falls as snow when the air temperature is below 2°C. It is a myth that it needs to be below zero to snow. In fact the heaviest snow falls tend to occur when the air temperature is between zero and 2°C. The falling snow does begin to melt as soon as the temperature rises above freezing, but as the melting process begins, the air around the snowflake is cooled.

If the temperature is warmer than 2°C then the snowflake will melt and fall as sleet rather than snow, and if it's warmer still, it will be rain.

The size and make up of a snowflake depends on how many ice crystals group together, and this will be determined by air temperatures. Snowflakes that fall through dry, cool air will be small, powdery snowflakes that don't stick together. This 'dry' snow is ideal for snow sports but is more likely to drift in windy weather.

When the temperature is slightly warmer than 0°C, the snowflakes will melt around the edges and stick together to become big, heavy flakes. This creates 'wet' snow, which sticks together easily and is good for making snowmen.

Which of the following statements about snow match the information in the passage?

○ A Snow is formed from ice.

○ B Falling snow melts because of warm air around it.

○ C Subzero temperatures are required for snow to fall.

○ D Sleet develops at less than two degrees centigrade.

○ E Dry snow falls in colder temperatures than wet snow.

❷ **Read the text and answer the question by selecting all the correct responses.** ***You will need to select more than one response.***

Water for public supply can be obtained from underground sources by wells sunk into aquifers, or from surface sources, such as purpose-built reservoirs or lakes (collecting rainwater run-off or water from streams) and rivers. The safety of the water is of utmost concern – several million people die each year after consuming contaminated water. The primary aim in water treatment is the elimination of any pathogenic micro-organisms present. All the above-mentioned sources can be subject to pollution. In the case of underground water, polluted surface water can enter the saturation zone of an aquifer and so lead to its contamination. Pollution can come from waste containing heavy metals and organic compounds, farm run-off containing pesticides, and industrial wastes which may have been deliberately dumped down old coal mine shafts. River water can be affected by farm drainage, sewage works and industrial effluents, and also the run-off water from roads. Thus there is a need to maintain the quality of the aquatic environment to ensure that the water is suitable for treatment for public supply, and that the cost of treatment is kept as low as possible.

Raw water is usually abstracted from a river and pumped to a reservoir for storage and settlement. In the reservoir, the number of bacteria is reduced through natural processes, such as ultraviolet radiation from sunlight. Also, a large portion of the suspended solids settles out. The water is then conveyed from the reservoir to a treatment works.

Which of the following statements are true according to the information in the passage?

○ A There are insufficient sources of fresh water for human consumption.

○ B Industrial pollution can affect both underground and river water.

○ C There are numerous means by which water can become impure.

○ D Rain is a safer source of water for human consumption than aquifers.

○ E Water in reservoirs is chemically treated to remove harmful bacteria.

Re-order paragraphs

In the test, there are 2–3 tasks. For each task, you drag paragraphs from the left and drop them into the correct order on the right. The wording in the instructions below is the same as you will see in the actual test. See page 35 for help.

The text boxes in the left panel have been placed in a random order. Restore the original order by dragging the text boxes from the left panel to the right panel.

1

A One such example is a solar panel which could charge an LED lamp to create hours of light each day.

B In addition to being fairly costly, these create smoke pollution and carbon emissions.

C Therefore, alternatives are being investigated.

D A result of not being connected to the electricity grid in rural areas of some countries means people light their homes using kerosene lamps.

2

A The fear of criticism from colleagues, friends and family is the main factor that obstructs a change in their employment situation.

B However, most of these workers would not consider career alternatives.

C It seems that the lack of psychological reward is the reason for their dissatisfaction.

D Despite the financial stability a high salary brings, research has shown that the majority of top earners are not happy in their jobs.

E Interestingly, it is not the risk of a decrease in salary which prevents this move.

Reading: Fill in the blanks

In the test, there are 4–5 tasks. For each task, you drag the words at the bottom of the text and drop them into the correct space in the text. The wording in the instructions below is the same as you will see in the actual test. See page 37 for help.

In the text below some words are missing. Drag words from the box below to the appropriate place in the text. To undo an answer choice, drag the word back to the box below the text.

❶ Using questionnaires to gather information from people is a well-used quantitative research method. It is considered to be an easy [1] ______, but in reality it is actually very difficult to design a good questionnaire. Question type, clarity of language, length of questionnaire and layout are just some of the many [2] ______, which all need to be carefully considered when designing the questionnaire. Another issue, which [3] ______ some deliberation, is how to ensure a high response [4] ______.

option | opportunity | selection | influences | requires | factors | rate

❷ Psychology is a suitable course of study for those [1] ______ in all aspects of human thought and behaviour. It can be [2] ______ as the scientific study of how humans function on a biological, social and mental level. There are a range of influential approaches to the subject, which are [3] ______ to such areas as child development, health, education and sports.

practised | defined | affected | interested | applied | diagnosed

❸ Migration could be described as the well-defined journey animals make to a familiar [1] ______ at specific seasons or times of the year. All species that migrate do so for a common [2] ______, in order to survive. Migration allows them to spend their life in more than one area and thus [3] ______ problems that can occur in one habitat, such as lack of food, shelter or exposure to harsh weather.

position | purpose | destination | experience | situation | avoid

❹ Multinational companies are often criticised for a number of reasons, but we cannot deny their [1] ______ impact. Employment opportunities are generated for locals in the overseas country. When multinational companies set up manufacturing plants, there is often an increased [2] ______ of products for local consumers, which profits the local economy. Training is also sometimes provided in the use of technology; moreover, the experience and knowledge that the employees [3] ______ strengthens their skills and overall employability.

positive | gain | purchase | negative | availability | benefit

Reading & writing: Fill in the blanks

In the test, there are 5–6 tasks. For each task, you have a text with several gaps. You select the correct answer for each gap from the drop-down list on the screen. The wording in the instructions below is the same as you will see in the actual test. See page 40 for help.

Below is a text with blanks. Click on each blank, a list of choices will appear. Select the appropriate choice for each blank.

1 A well-known feature of the European landscape is the castle. Some types of fortifications [1] ______ built thousands of years ago, but the first real castles only started to appear as recently as one thousand years ago. Construction of most of the larger castles in Europe was between around 1100 and 1500. Initially, the [2] ______ of these castles was to lay claim to land won in battle and also for defence. [3] ______, the owners of the castles also realised that their castles were an effective [4] ______ to intimidate local people. Therefore, castles became a symbol of wealth and authority for those owning them, and a useful tool to keep control of territory and the residents living on that territory.

1	A have been	B were	C have	D was
2	A purpose	B feature	C aspect	D plan
3	A Alternatively	B Fortunately	C However	D Thus
4	A process	B form	C way	D use

2 A recent study reveals that the ability to walk quickly in old age is an indicator of a long life. The report examined results from recent research. The [1] ______ in the research were tested on a regular [2] ______ over an extended period of time. The researchers focused on the relationship between walking speed in the post sixty-five age group and longevity. They concluded that there was a direct correlation between walking speed and life span.

A key researcher gave the explanation that this link exists [3] ______ walking involves the use of many bodily functions working in unison. The heart, lungs, skeletal system, joints, muscles, nerves and brain have to work together in order to ensure a consistent speed. Damage to any of these systems may mean a much slower walking speed [4] ______ could signal medical problems.

1	A experimenters	B investigators	C performers	D participants
2	A circumstance	B situation	C condition	D basis
3	A therefore	B instead of	C because	D so
4	A which	B also	C this	D it

TEST 3

READING

Below is a text with blanks. Click on each blank, a list of choices will appear. Select the appropriate answer for each blank.

3 One of the questions we need to ask ourselves is: How much of the news is biased? Can we recognise bias? The fact is, despite the journalistic ideal of 'objectivity', every news story is [1] ______ by the attitudes and background of its interviewers, writers, journalists, photographers and editors. That is not to say that all bias is [2] ______, but it does exist.

So how can we, as readers or viewers, determine bias? Well, in the case of newspapers, it manifests itself in a number of ways, such as what events [3] ______ for inclusion or omission. The [4] ______ of the article, meaning its proximity to the front or back pages, is significant. The use of headlines, photographs and language are further examples.

1	A influenced	B agreed	C judged	D fixed
2	A considered	B accidental	C deliberate	D balanced
3	A being selected	B have selected	C are selected	D selected
4	A placement	B space	C area	D size

4 It is believed that the only purpose of advertising is to make people buy something. It is undeniable that this is the ultimate, overall goal, but there are [1] ______ equally essential, yet more subtle, aims of an advert as well. For example, people may not buy something as a result of an advert, but that advert [2] ______ awareness of that product and brand. Sufficient advertising will reinforce that awareness [3] ______ when people purchase something, they may choose the heavily advertised brand that can be easily remembered over others; purely on the basis that they may have heard or seen that name and they are not as [4] ______ with the other names or brands available.

1	A necessary	B another	C other	D more
2	A will have improved	B will be improved	C was improved	D is improved
3	A except	B but	C yet	D so
4	A memorable	B familiar	C common	D known

Below is a text with blanks. Click on each blank, a list of choices will appear. Select the appropriate answer for each blank.

5 Sixty years ago an American sociologist made a distinction between 'private troubles' and 'public issues'. His theory was that [1] ______ there being many 'troubles' or 'problems' that individuals may experience in their lives, not all of these always emerge as 'public issues' which attract general interest, or are seen as requiring public responses or even action. Personal troubles are seen as 'private' and are [2] ______ within households, families or maybe even small communities. On the other hand, 'public issues' are dealt with publicly, through forms of social intervention or regulation, for example. One [3] ______ that distinguishes whether issues or problems are perceived as private or public is number. [4] ______ only a few people experience some form of trouble, then it is highly likely to remain a private matter; whereas when a large number of people begin to experience this same trouble it will quite possibly [5] ______ a public issue.

1	A otherwise	B although	C besides	D despite
2	A handled	B effected	C advised	D applied
3	A influence	B reason	C effect	D factor
4	A Consequently	B Whether	C Either	D If
5	A become	B involve	C remain	D stay

Summarize spoken text

In the test, there are 2–3 tasks. For each task, you listen to the audio then type your summary into the box on the screen. The wording in the instructions below is the same as you will see in the actual test. See page 45 for help.

You will hear a short lecture. Write a summary for a fellow student who was not present at the lecture. You should write 50–70 words.

10 min. You will have 10 minutes to finish this task. Your response will be judged on the quality of your writing and on how well your response presents the key points presented in the lecture.

1 ▸ 105

....

....

....

....

....

....

2 ▸ 106

....

....

....

....

....

....

Multiple-choice, choose multiple answers

In the test, there are 2–3 tasks. For each task, you listen to the audio then click the buttons next to all of the answers you think are correct. The wording in the instructions below is the same as you will see in the actual test. See page 47 for help.

Listen to the recording and answer the question by selecting all the correct responses. *You will need to select more than one response.*

1 ▶ 107 The purposes of this talk are to

- ○ A explain how humans grade writing.
- ○ B present different methods for grading writing.
- ○ C criticize the use of technology in grading writing.
- ○ D describe the findings of a research project.
- ○ E suggest directions for future research.

2 ▶ 108 What does the speaker say about sharks?

- ○ A They are hunted heavily because their price is high.
- ○ B They are a more popular food source than other fish species.
- ○ C They reproduce more slowly than other fish do.
- ○ D They live for much longer than other species of fish.
- ○ E They are more likely to become extinct than other fish.

Fill in the blanks

In the test, there are 2–3 tasks. For each task, there is a text with several gaps. You type the correct answer for each gap into the box in the text. The wording in the instructions below is the same as you will see in the actual test. See page 49 for help.

You will hear a recording. Type the missing words in each blank.

1 ▶ 109

To be honest, the biggest problem for most undergraduate students, in terms of academic writing, is not only adapting to a far more [1] ______ and formal style, but also learning how to ascertain the difference between important, [2] ______ information and unnecessary, or even irrelevant [3] ______. In my experience, I would say it takes students their first year, if not longer, to [4] ______ what is required and to start to implement those requirements in their writing. What they really should be doing, if they are struggling with written [5] ______, is to seek help from the [6] ______ support services which are available at the University.

2 ▶ 110

An important question about education is, then, why do some types of students achieve success easily and others struggle to do well? Well, one theory is that there is a [1] ______ reason for academic achievement. What I mean by that is, a certain innate, measurable level of [2] ______. Another frequently discussed theory is environmental factors, such as the effect of home and family upbringing. A final reason is related to the teaching and learning [3] ______ within educational institutions, and the way it is organized, administered and [4] ______.

TEST 3 LISTENING

Highlight correct summary

In the test, there are 2–3 tasks. For each task, you listen to the audio then click the button next to the summary you think is correct. The wording in the instructions below is the same as you will see in the actual test. See page 51 for help.

You will hear a recording. Click on the paragraph that best relates to the recording.

1 ▶ 111

○ A Research into family history by ordinary people only started to become far more widespread in the early nineteenth century. Prior to that time, it was chiefly rich, important and powerful families who had an interest and involvement in this type of activity.

○ B The study of family history began hundreds of years ago in North Africa in order to establish such things as ownership of property. It rapidly became a common practice in many cultures because inheritance played such an important role in society and government.

○ C Originally, tracing family history was only used in order to establish the origins of prosperous and powerful families. However, by the middle of the twentieth century, ordinary people were also starting to show an interest in researching their family background too.

○ D All social classes of the general population have always been interested in recording their family history, but genealogy became really popular in the early nineteenth century due to the publication of a book concerned with methodology of determining family history.

TEST 3

LISTENING

You will hear a recording. Click on the paragraph that best relates to the recording.

2 ▸ 112

○ A Anthropologists have disagreed for some time regarding when and how fire was first used in prehistoric times. Recent findings have now managed to finally persuade them that it was used before they thought and the principle use of fire was for cooking rather than any other purpose.

○ B Scientists believe they are now nearer to finding an answer to the question of when humans first started to use fire, and it is much earlier than had been thought. Nevertheless, there is still some disagreement among researchers around what early humans actually used the fire for.

○ C There has been much discussion by anthropologists about when humans started to use fires. As a result of a recent discovery it is thought that they started to make fires 300,000 years ago, but the reason they made them is still not clear.

○ D Recent findings have convinced the anthropological community that previous conclusions from research done over many decades was correct in estimating when early humans started to use fire although this research was incorrect in its findings about what fire was used for.

Multiple-choice, choose single answer

In the test, there are 2–3 tasks. For each task, you listen to the audio then click the button next to the answer you think is correct. The wording in the instructions below is the same as you will see in the actual test. See page 54 for help.

Listen to the recording and answer the multiple-choice question by selecting the correct response. *Only one response is correct.*

1 ▶ 113 What does the speaker say about dissertations?

- ○ A They are too difficult for students to do.
- ○ B The subject area selected may not have sufficient focus.
- ○ C There is a lack of understanding of how to conduct research.
- ○ D Students will not be allowed to alter their proposed topic.

2 ▶ 114 What is an important rationale for art therapy?

- ○ A Patients are able to develop an artistic skill.
- ○ B Therapists can diagnose problems more successfully.
- ○ C It is the most effective psychological therapy.
- ○ D It is suitable for less orally communicative patients.

Select missing word

In the test, there are 2–3 tasks. For each task, you listen to the audio then click the button next to the words you think complete the audio. The wording in the instructions below is the same as you will see in the actual test. See page 56 for help.

1 ▶ 115 You will hear a recording about an archaeological discovery. *At the end of the recording the last word or group of words has been replaced by a beep.* Select the correct option to complete the recording.

○ A are much older than expected

○ B could very possibly be fake

○ C belonged to that culture

2 ▶ 116 You will hear a recording about measuring time. *At the end of the recording the last word or group of words has been replaced by a beep.* Select the correct option to complete the recording.

○ A ancient civilisations

○ B desert tribes

○ C historical periods

○ D current days

Highlight incorrect words

In the test, there are 2–3 tasks. For each task, you listen to the audio and follow the words in the text on the screen. You click on the words that are different on the screen and the audio. The wording in the instructions below is the same as you will see in the actual test. See page 58 for help.

You will hear a recording. Below is a transcription of the recording. *Some words in the transcription differ from what the speaker said.* Please click on the words that are different.

1 ▶ 117 Transcription:

One of the most encouraging phenomena in recent years has been the development of lifelong learning in the education sector. Nowadays, students are embarking on courses at all ages. Higher education is no longer viewed as a place for the young. Mature students are appreciated and respected. Recent research has also indicated that older students are dedicated learners, able to contribute a number of skills and talents gained from work, family and other life experiences.

2 ▶ 118 Transcription:

Conducting a video conference is now a popular method of communication in the business world. This telecommunications technology allows two or more locations to communicate by simultaneous video and audio transmissions. It's designed to serve conferences or meetings in many locations.

The advantages are obvious: no more lengthy phone calls or complicated correspondence with business contacts, partners or offices abroad. This relatively low cost, fast, effective communication method has made significant inroads in not just a business environment, but also education, medicine and media.

Write from dictation

In the test, there are 3–4 tasks. For each task, you listen and type the sentence you hear into the box on the screen. The wording in the instructions below is the same as you will see in the actual test. See page 60 for help.

You will hear a sentence. Type the sentence in the box below exactly as you hear it. Write as much of the sentence as you can. You will hear the sentence only once.

1 ▶ 119

....

....

....

2 ▶ 120

....

....

....

3 ▶ 121

....

....

....

TEST 3

LISTENING

TEST 4

Read aloud

In the test, there are 6–7 tasks. For each task, you read the text aloud into the microphone. The wording in the instructions below is the same as you will see in the actual test. See page 12 for help.

40 sec. **Look at the text below. In 40 seconds, you must read this text aloud as naturally and as clearly as possible. You have 40 seconds to read aloud.**

1 The Italian alphabet has fewer letters in comparison with the English alphabet. Italian does not use the letters J, K, W, X or Y – except in borrowed words. However, young Italians are increasingly using the letter K in words that would be written with C or CH in standard Italian orthography.

2 Summerhill School was regarded with considerable suspicion by the educational establishment. Lessons were optional for pupils at the school, and the government of the school was carried out by a School Council, of which all the pupils and staff were members, with everyone having equal voting rights.

3 This term the University is running a series of workshops for final year students on how to do well in interviews. These sessions will help participants prepare effectively for – and perform at their best during – later job interviews. The workshop tutors have an excellent record of success in helping students acquire the positions they desire.

4 Tasmania is a large and relatively sparsely populated island off the south coast of Australia. The island is of particular interest to natural scientists, who go there to research the unique wildlife. Tasmania has, for example, twelve species of bird that are not found anywhere else in the world.

5 Honey has traditionally been credited with significant medical powers, and it has played a major part in many folk remedies. But it seems now its efficacy is not just an old wives' tale. Recent research has shown there is scientific evidence to prove that honey contains elements that prevent bacteria from growing.

6 The College has a fascinating museum dedicated to archaeology and anthropology. It contains information about many of the studies which have been carried out by members of the College over the five hundred years of its existence. There are many unique exhibits brought back from excavations and explorations in all the continents.

Repeat sentence

In the test, there are 10–12 tasks. For each task, you listen and repeat the sentence you hear into the microphone. The wording in the instructions below is the same as you will see in the actual test. See page 14 for help.

▸ 122–131 15 sec. You will hear a sentence. Please repeat the sentence exactly as you hear it. You will hear the sentence only once.

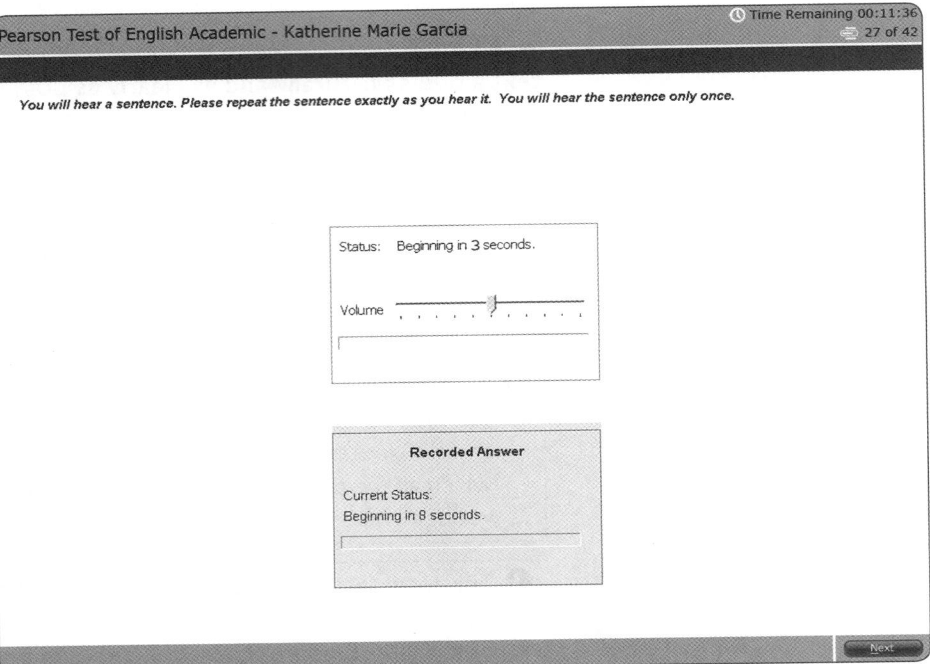

Repeat sentence: Each question is displayed on a new screen.

Describe image

In the test, there are 6–7 tasks. For each task, you look at the image and describe it into the microphone. The wording in the instructions below is the same as you will see in the actual test. See page 16 for help.

1 40 sec. Look at the map below. In 25 seconds, please speak into the microphone and describe in detail what the map is showing. You will have 40 seconds to give your response.

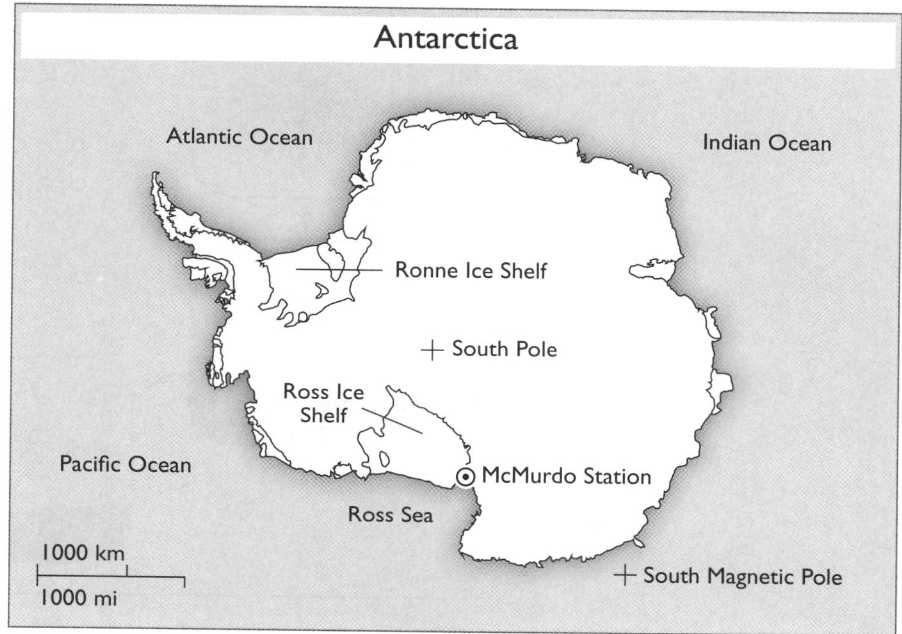

2 40 sec. Look at the graph below. In 25 seconds, please speak into the microphone and describe in detail what the graph is showing. You will have 40 seconds to give your response.

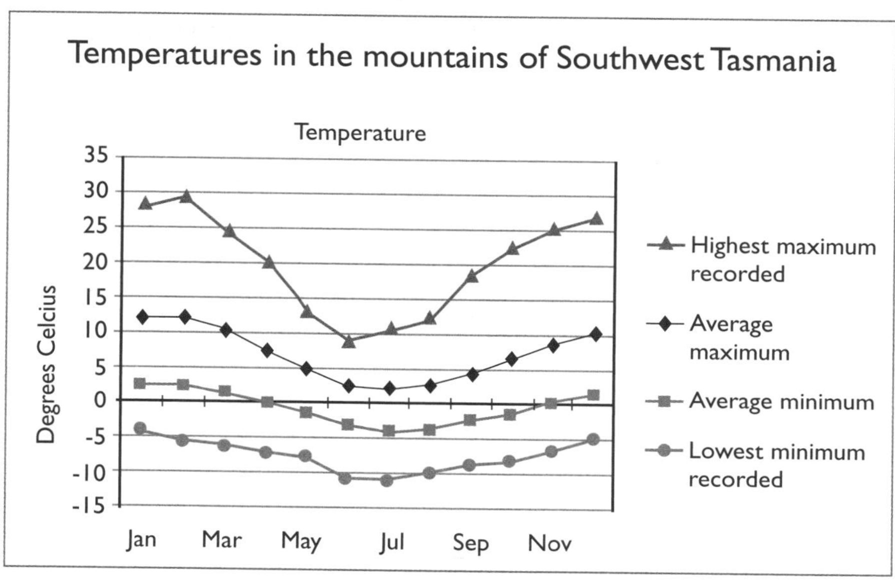

TEST 4 SPEAKING

3 40 sec. Look at the diagram below. In 25 seconds, please speak into the microphone and describe in detail what the diagram is showing. You will have 40 seconds to give your response.

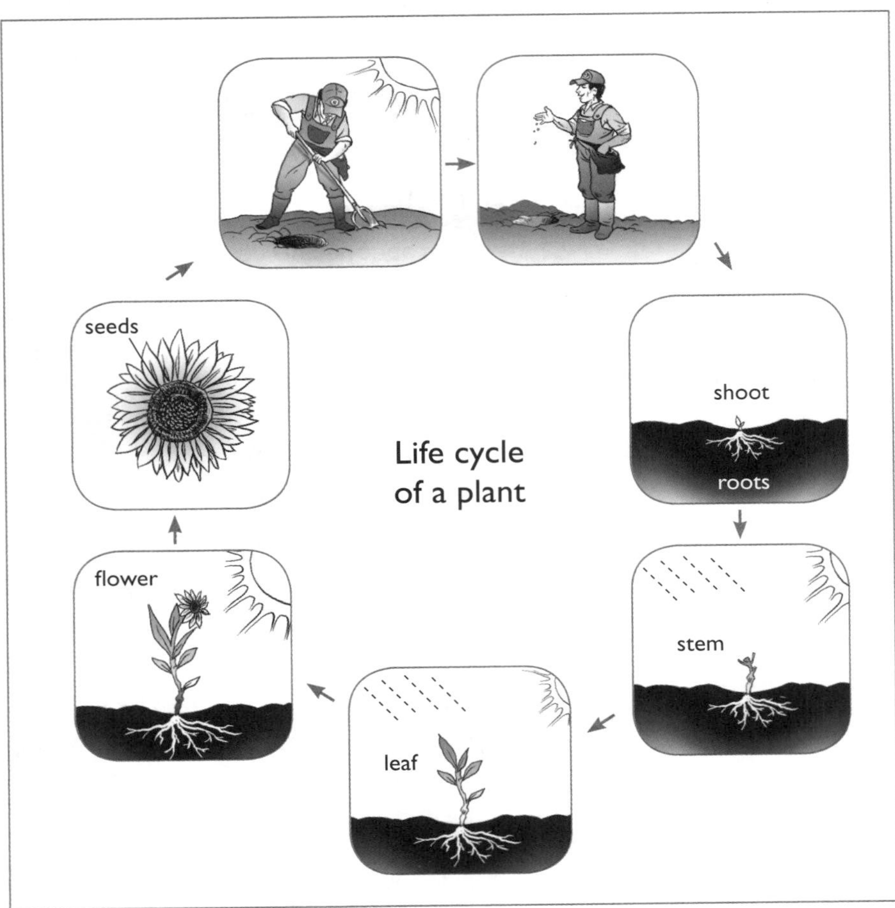

4 40 sec. Look at the table below. In 25 seconds, please speak into the microphone and describe in detail what the table is showing. You will have 40 seconds to give your response.

Export of motorcycles from Japan

Last calendar year, by region (%)

	Share (%)	% change on previous year
Asia	7.7	-4.7
Middle East	0.7	-2.9
Europe	34.5	-23.6
North America	35.5	+68.7
Central America	1.2	+11.6
South America	8.0	+19.9
Africa	4.2	-17.8
Oceania	8.2	-16.7
Total	*100.0*	+2.3

TEST 4

SPEAKING

5 40 sec. Look at the chart below. In 25 seconds, please speak into the microphone and describe in detail what the chart is showing. You will have 40 seconds to give your response.

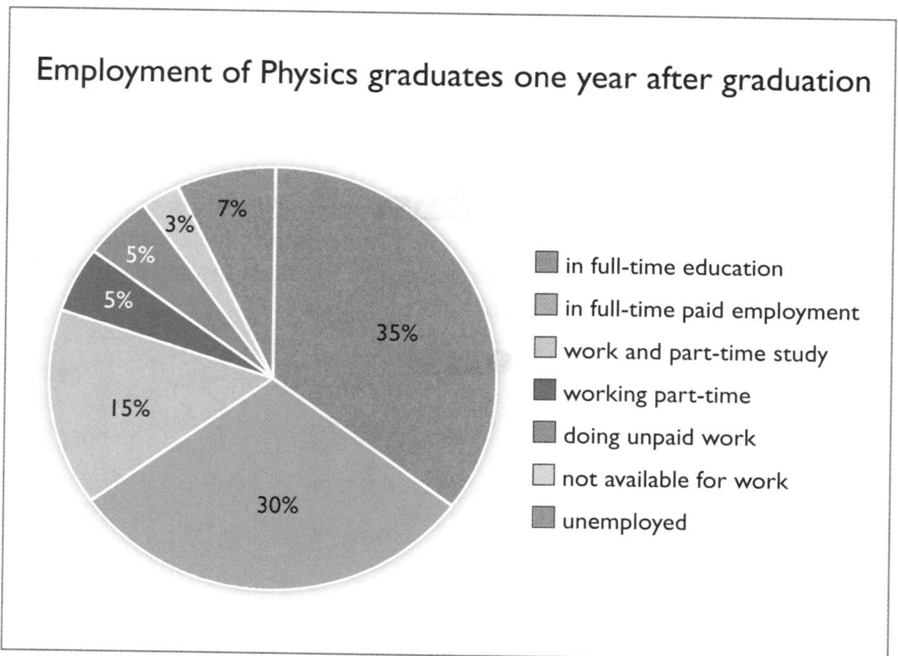

6 40 sec. Look at the chart below. In 25 seconds, please speak into the microphone and describe in detail what the chart is showing. You will have 40 seconds to give your response.

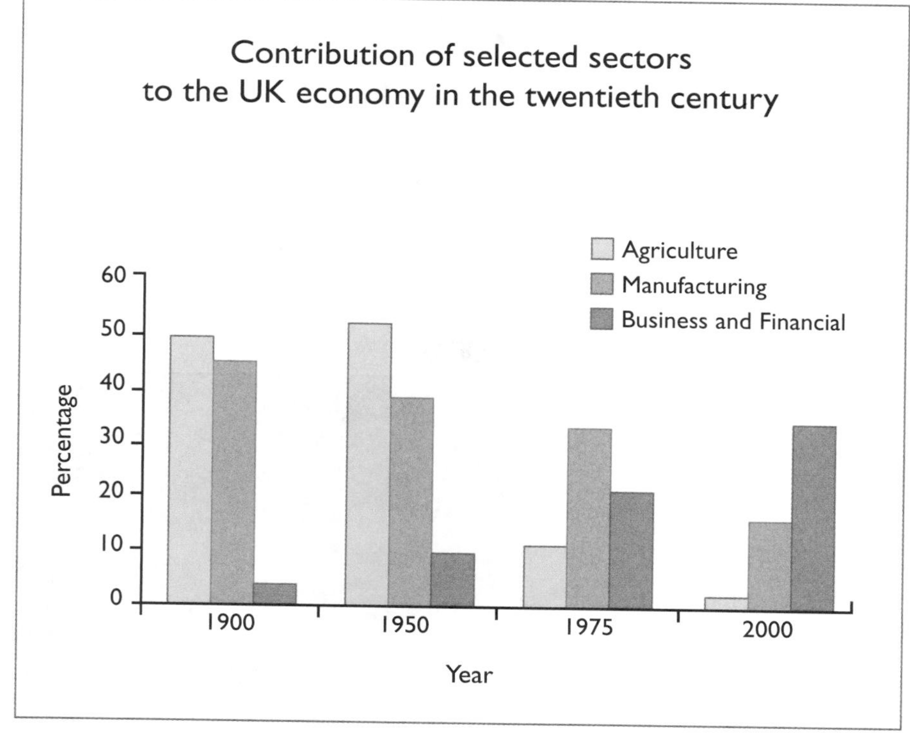

TEST 4 SPEAKING

Re-tell lecture

In the test, there are 3–4 tasks. For each task, you see an image on the screen. Listen to the lecture and then speak into the microphone. The wording in the instructions below is the same as you will see in the actual test. See page 20 for help.

40 sec. You will hear a lecture. After listening to the lecture, in 10 seconds, please speak into the microphone and retell what you have just heard from the lecture in your own words. You will have 40 seconds to give your response.

1  132

2 ▸ 133

3 ▸ 134

Answer short question

In the test, there are 10–12 tasks. For each task, you hear a question and speak your answer into the microphone. The wording in the instructions below is the same as you will see in the actual test. See page 22 for help.

▸ 135–144 10 sec. You will hear a question. Please give a simple and short answer. Often just one or a few words is enough.

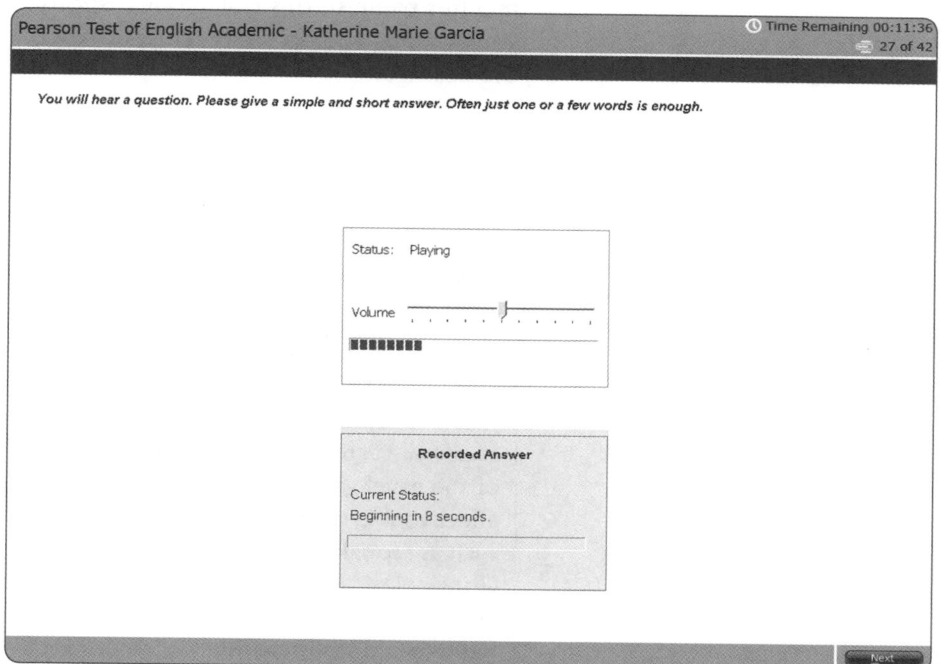

Answer short question: Each question is displayed on a new screen.

Summarize written text

In the test, there are 2–3 tasks. Each task has a text on the screen. You type your summary of the text into the box at the bottom of the screen. The wording in the instructions below is the same as you will see in the actual test. See page 24 for help.

1 **10 min.** **Read the passage below and summarize it using one sentence. Type your response in the box at the bottom of the screen. You have 10 minutes to finish this task. Your response will be judged on the quality of your writing and on how well your response presents the key points in the passage.**

Times are fraught, and overstretched executives are constantly on the lookout for a way to clear their minds so they can work in a calmer, more effective, and more responsive way. Cultivating a special state of consciousness called 'mindfulness' – an intense awareness of the here and now – is proving attractive to a growing number of senior managers, both in the US and elsewhere.

Mindfulness is achieved by meditation techniques, often involving sitting on a cushion, eyes closed, concentrating on the inflow and outflow of your breath. Or you might spend 10 minutes studying, sniffing, tasting and finally eating a piece of fruit. That might make it sound like a remnant of the navel-gazing 1960s and 1970s, but the evidence for mindfulness's effectiveness is good enough to have impressed hard-nosed companies such as Google (which has invited mindfulness gurus to speak at the Googleplex), General Mills, PricewaterhouseCoopers, Deutsche Bank, Procter & Gamble, AstraZeneca, Apple, Credit Suisse, KPMG, Innocent, Reuters and many more.

According to Don McCormick, assistant professor of management at California State University and a dedicated meditator, it 'can help individuals to manage workplace stress, perform tasks more effectively, enhance self-awareness and self-regulation, experience work as more meaningful, improve workplace relationships, increase ethical behavior, and make perception more accurate'. It is said to pay dividends for leaders and managers, by improving the quality of their listening and communicating.

....

....

....

....

....

2 10 min. **Read the passage below and summarize it using one sentence. Type your response in the box at the bottom of the screen. You have 10 minutes to finish this task. Your response will be judged on the quality of your writing and on how well your response presents the key points in the passage.**

One of the many critiques of academic research that one runs across is that a lot of research done by a faculty at universities across America doesn't 'do' anything: it doesn't lead to some new product that can be marketed; it doesn't create jobs; it doesn't have an obvious social value. After all, people argue, do we really need studies that chart the maturation of catfish? Or that explore the nuances of a minor poet? What is all this for?

As a consequence of attitudes like these, many people – particularly politicians and business persons – argue that the research function should be stripped from academia, or at least those parts of academia that aren't the major research institutions. Then universities wouldn't need so many faculties, and costs could be contained.

Academics like me offer lots of standard objections to this line of thinking: that research keeps one fresh and up-to-date in the discipline; that the faculty often works with students on their research, thus providing students with invaluable training for their future careers and so on.

All of this is true, but I want to add a different point: the power of chance.

In 1990, I took an appointment at the University of Alabama-Huntsville. I had a police officer student who invited me for a ride along. I went – ultimately many times. The book that emerged from the research project I established from that first ride was later included on a list of 'must read' books on public administration by the Government of Canada.

I have no problem with accountability. But if you had asked me what my purpose was when I took my first ride along, and you had demanded to know what use the research could be put to, I would have told you, 'I have no idea'.

....

....

....

....

....

3 10 min. Read the passage below and summarize it using one sentence. Type your response in the box at the bottom of the screen. You have 10 minutes to finish this task. Your response will be judged on the quality of your writing and on how well your response presents the key points in the passage.

Current research into the nature of the relationship between participation in physical activity/sport and educational performance has produced mixed, inconsistent and often non-comparable results. For example, some cross-sectional studies illustrate a positive correlation between participation in sport and physical activity and academic success (e.g. maths, reading, acuity, reaction times). However, critics point to a general failure to solve the issue of direction of cause – whether intelligence leads to success in sport, whether involvement in sport enhances academic performance, or whether a third factor (e.g. personality traits) explains both.

Longitudinal studies also generally support the suggestion that academic performance is enhanced, or at least maintained, by increased habitual physical activity. Yet such studies are criticized for not being definitive because some do not use randomised allocation of pupils to experimental and control groups (to control for pre-existing differences), others tend to use (subjective) teacher-assigned grades to assess academic achievement, rather than standardised and comparable tests; and some programmes include parallel interventions, making it difficult to isolate specific effects.

More generically, one key piece of research illustrates that both acute exercise and chronic training programmes have small, but beneficial, positive impacts on cognitive performance. However, this study concludes that as experimental rigour decreased, effect size increased. Further, generalisation is limited because effect size is influenced by the nature and type of exercise, the type of participants, the nature of the cognitive tests and the methodological quality of the study.

....

....

....

....

....

Write essay

In the test, there are 1–2 tasks. For each task, the essay question is on the screen. You type your essay into the box on the screen. The wording in the instructions below is the same as you will see in the actual test. See page 27 for help.

20 min. You will have 20 minutes to plan, write and revise an essay about the topic below. Your response will be judged on how well you develop a position, organize your ideas, present supporting details, and control the elements of standard written English. You should write 200–300 words.

> 'Computer technology has had more of a negative than a positive impact on society.'
>
> How far do you agree with this statement? Support your views with reasons and/or examples from your own experience.

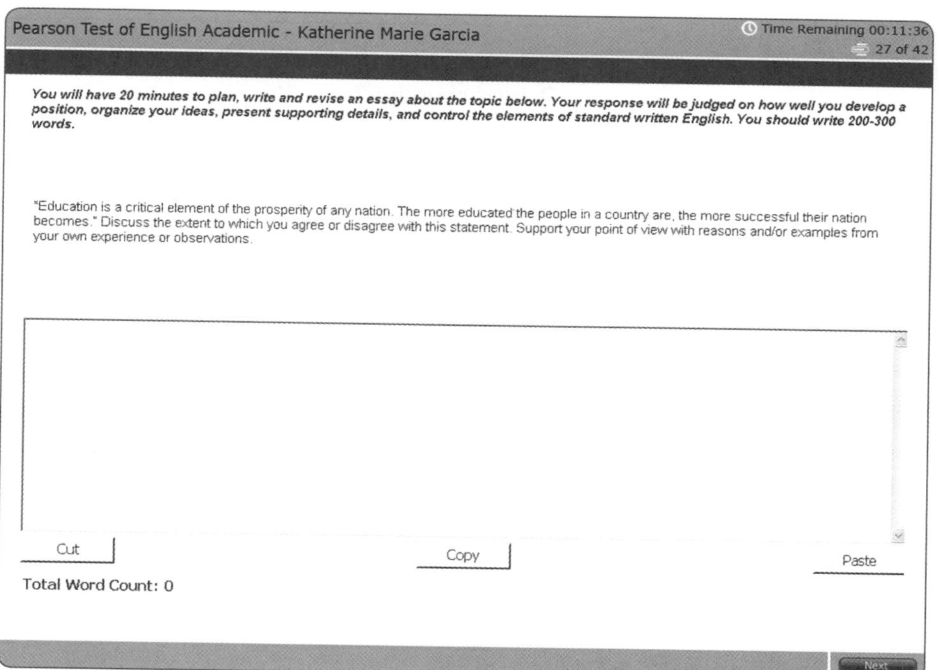

Write essay: Each question is displayed on a new screen.

Multiple-choice, choose single answer

In the test, there are 2–3 tasks. For each task, you read the text on the left of the screen and look at the options on the right of the screen. You click the button next to the answer you think is correct. The wording in the instructions below is the same as you will see in the actual test. See page 30 for help.

Read the text and answer the multiple-choice question by selecting the correct response. ***Only one response is correct.***

1 It is a curious tradition that the clock on the tower of Christ Church Cathedral in Oxford is always five minutes later than standard British time. The explanation for this lies in the conservative nature of the Cathedral's clergy. It was only when the railways arrived in the middle of the nineteenth century that it became important for clocks throughout the country to be synchronised, however difficult this might be. When the Cathedral was asked to come into line, the clergy discussed the request but decided that this was an idea that needed to prove its worth before being adopted.

Why does Christ Church Cathedral clock give a different time from other British churches?

- ○ A Oxford likes to be different from other places.
- ○ B It was initially a protest against the coming of the railway.
- ○ C Cathedral staff were reluctant to act too quickly.
- ○ D It was very difficult to alter the time on the clock.

2 Zebras are members of the horse family. However, these 'stripey horses' are not used for riding. Keen riders have occasionally attempted to try. Although zebras have at times let someone sit on their back, the rider soon discovered that a zebra's neck is stiffer than a horse's, lacking the suppleness that enables riders to control the horse. The structure of a zebra's back also makes it less suitable for riding. It would undoubtedly be possible to breed zebras that would ride well, but with the arrival of the internal combustion engine there has not been much incentive to do so.

What is the writer's conclusion about zebras?

- ○ A Zebras are not as similar to horses as they initially appear.
- ○ B People have little motivation to develop a zebra that could be ridden.
- ○ C It is unlikely that people could develop a zebra that would be good to ride.
- ○ D Motorised vehicles are gradually reducing the numbers of zebras that are being bred.

Multiple-choice, choose multiple answers

In the test, there are 2–3 tasks. For each task, you read the text on the left of the screen and look at the options on the right of the screen. You click the buttons next to all of the answers you think are correct. The wording in the instructions below is the same as you will see in the actual test. See page 32 for help.

1 **Read the text and answer the question by selecting all the correct responses.** *You will need to select more than one response.*

> Much has been written on the wooden sculptures of West Africa, especially Nigeria, which was pre-eminent in the art, for unlike other crafts, wood-carving has long been acknowledged in the West as an art form. Yet, compared with stone or bronze, wood is not a very durable material in tropical conditions and the oldest carvings in Nigeria are probably no more than two hundred and fifty years old. Many of the earliest, maybe the finest of the wood carvings may also have been destroyed by termites. When one is attacked in this way, no attempt is made to preserve it; a new one is made to replace it, for the creativity of making it is valued above the object *per se*. The finest sculptures were made for religious or ceremonial purposes, and the art of creation was itself a religious act.

What has led to there being no very old wood carvings in West Africa?

- ○ A the nature of the climate there
- ○ B Western collectors' desire for such carvings
- ○ C the fact that other materials were used previously
- ○ D destruction of the carvings because of religion
- ○ E problems caused by insects

❷ Read the text and answer the question by selecting all the correct responses. *You will need to select more than one response.*

It is possible to study the curriculum of an educational institution from a number of different perspectives. In the first instance, we can look at curriculum planning, that is at decision-making, in relation to identifying learners' needs and purposes; establishing goals and objectives; selecting and grading content; organising appropriate learning arrangements and learner groupings; selecting, adapting or developing appropriate materials, learning tasks and assessment and evaluation tools.

Alternatively, we can study the curriculum in action, as it were. This second perspective takes us into the classroom itself. Here, we can observe the teaching/learning process and study the ways in which the intentions of the curriculum planners, which were developed during the planning phase, are put into action.

Yet another perspective relates to assessment and evaluation. From this perspective we would try and find out what students had learned and what they had failed to learn, in relation to what had been planned. In addition we might want to find out if they had learned anything which had not been planned.

Which of these ways of looking at an institution's curriculum is outlined in the text?

○ A observing what happens during lessons

○ B evaluating the materials used

○ C analysing the content of tests

○ D considering what is taken into account when preparing the curriculum

○ E comparing this curriculum with other choices that could have been made

○ F reviewing actual learning compared to curriculum goals

○ G assessing the effectiveness of teacher preparation for lessons

TEST 4 READING

Re-order paragraphs

In the test, there are 2–3 tasks. For each task, you drag paragraphs from the left and drop them into the correct order on the right. The wording in the instructions below is the same as you will see in the actual test. See page 35 for help.

The text boxes in the left panel have been placed in a random order. Restore the original order by dragging the text boxes from the left panel to the right panel.

1

A There you will see how women are consistently portrayed as weak and in need of male protection.

B This acceptance that men were the superior gender had not developed by chance.

C It had been the view that had been socialized into them from the moment of their birth.

D This will become clear if you look at any girls' magazine or popular film of the period.

E In the 1960s, the greatest obstacle for those who wanted to organize women was said to be women's conviction that they were actually inferior to men.

2

A It is mainly due to the quality of the fabric which effectively resists salt water, direct sunshine and cold winds.

B Traditionally they are navy blue and they are basically square in shape, without a curved armhole or inset sleeve.

C Fishermen's knitted jerseys have always been recognizable in Britain by their colour and their shape.

D This continuing popularity cannot just be put down to a fondness for tradition.

E These navy jerseys are still a familiar sight on any quay or harbour in the land.

Reading: Fill in the blanks

In the test, there are 4–5 tasks. For each task, you drag the words at the bottom of the text and drop them into the correct space in the text. The wording in the instructions below is the same as you will see in the actual test. See page 37 for help.

In the text below some words are missing. Drag words from the box below to the appropriate place in the text. To undo an answer choice, drag the word back to the box below the text.

1 There are two basic branches of the science of astronomy: observational and theoretical. Observational astronomy, as the name suggests, is concerned with observing the [1] ______ and then analyzing the observations, using the [2] ______ of physics. Theoretical astronomy focuses more on developing computer or analytical models to [3] ______ astronomical phenomena. The two [4] ______ complement each other, with observational astronomers attempting to [5] ______ theoretical results, and theoreticians aiming to explain what has been observed.

angles | confirm | describe | effects | fields | principles | reason | skies

2 Behanzin ruled the West African [1] ______ of Dahomey at the end of the nineteenth century, a time when Europeans were doing their utmost to colonise Africa. Behanzin put up extremely [2] ______ resistance. He did this with the [3] ______ of an army, including five thousand female warriors. He is often called King Shark, a name suggesting [4] ______ and wisdom. Famed for being a [5] ______ as well as a warrior, he wrote some of the most beautiful songs ever produced in Dahomey.

aid | battle | kingdom | light | poet | powerful | monarch | strength

3 An investigation into the study habits of undergraduates was carried out by a [1] ______ of researchers at a number of different universities. In all the universities [2] ______ in the study, it was found that there were the [3] ______ significant differences between the habits of arts and science students. Not surprisingly perhaps, arts students read more [4] ______, while science students tended to concentrate on a few [5] ______ texts.

core | heavily | involving | participating | same | staff | team | widely

4 Dolphins are marine mammals found all over the world. There are many [1] ______ species. They are well-known as intelligent creatures and seem to [2] ______ with one another in sophisticated ways. Dolphins are [3] ______ animals in that they live in groups. These can [4] ______ in size from five to several hundred. They often hunt in groups and work together to [5] ______ the fish or squid they like to eat.

capture | communicate | different | grow | learn | range | sociable | strange

Reading & writing: Fill in the blanks

In the test, there are 5–6 tasks. For each task, you have a text with several gaps. You select the correct answer for each gap from the drop-down list on the screen. The wording in the instructions below is the same as you will see in the actual test. See page 40 for help.

Below is a text with blanks. Click on each blank, a list of choices will appear. Select the appropriate choice for each blank.

1 Excavations have recently been carried out on an interesting Mayan house in Central America. The house dates [1] ______ the 9th century, and it has turned out to be of great interest to archaeologists. [2] ______ is particularly remarkable about the house is that its walls are covered with tables [3] ______ detailed astronomical calculations. These tables suggest that Mayan society had considerable understanding of astronomy at a much earlier time [4] ______ was previously thought to be the case. The tables focus on lunar cycles. This was important to the Mayans because they believed that there were six different gods of the moon, [5] ______ of which would take his turn to be in charge of the cycle at any given time.

1	A from	B to	C of	D by
2	A Which	B Where	C What	D Why
3	A showing	B showed	C shown	D show
4	A there	B that	C then	D than
5	A every	B most	C each	D all

2 Meteorologists are making increasing use of information provided on photo websites by ordinary people. There was a presentation dealing with [1] ______ they do this at a recent conference in New York. Scientists based at a university in Indiana looked at thousands of photos of snow scenes [2] ______ online. These provided them with information about snow falls in areas where, because of heavy cloud cover, [3] ______ information from satellite photography was available. It is not necessary to make use of this source of information as far as urban weather is [4] ______ , as there is usually easy access to plenty of other data about towns. But photos taken by the public can be an excellent way of filling in the gaps in knowledge [5] ______ weather events in more distant rural locations.

1	A whether	B what	C that	D how
2	A posting	B posted	C posts	D post
3	A some	B much	C any	D no
4	A concerning	B regarding	C concerned	D regarded
5	A about	B with	C for	D on

Below is a text with blanks. Click on each blank, a list of choices will appear. Select the appropriate choice for each blank.

3 A manakin is an unusual type of bird found in the tropical forests of Colombia and Ecuador. Approximately twenty of the forty different types of manakin [1] ______ a kind of music by moving their body parts. This is particularly done by the male bird when it is hoping to attract a female. Although ornithologists had [2] ______ been aware that the bird somehow managed to make its characteristic noise with its wings, they were unable to work out exactly how the sound was produced. [3] ______, a post-graduate student has recently solved the puzzle. She did so by recording the bird's movements with a camera operating [4] ______ a speed of a thousand frames per second. A standard camcorder records about 30 frames per second. On examining the footage she was able to see that the bird used one special feather to click against other feathers – in much the same way [5] ______ guitarists use a plectrum to pluck the strings of their instrument.

1	A make	B have	C get	D do
2	A once	B ever	C still	D long
3	A However	B Accordingly	C Moreover	D Whereas
4	A for	B by	C at	D in
5	A than	B like	C as	D so

4 A team of young engineering students in Japan are working on the production of a robotic suit. This [1] ______ been designed to help the elderly to move around and lift heavy objects [2] ______ easily. The suit is like a kind of exoskeleton which goes over the top of your body from your shoulders to your calves. It is made of aluminium and has joints at the shoulder and elbow. It is also equipped with artificial muscles. The wearer [3] ______ be helped to stand up, for example, by pressing controls which inject air into the suit [4] ______ that the legs straighten and the person rises. The suit weighs almost ten kilos but users report that this does not seem heavy at all. They said that the increased strength that they got [5] ______ wearing it gave them very positive feelings of empowerment.

1	A was	B has	C had	D is
2	A much	B more	C too	D far
3	A ought to	B used to	C must	D can
4	A until	B on	C so	D by
5	A after	B from	C with	D for

Below is a text with blanks. Click on each blank, a list of choices will appear. Select the appropriate choice for each blank.

5 Throughout history poetry has often been created to celebrate a wedding. This article will examine the ways in [1] ______ this has happened at different periods of time and in many [2] ______ differing societies. It will look at some examples of wedding poems from a range of eras and cultures, and will [3] ______ them in their specific context, drawing out the particular features that reflect that context. Other writers on this topic have tended to focus on more personal wedding poems, [4] ______ dedicated to the bride or the groom. Here, however, the intention is to consider poems that were written with more of a social purpose [5] ______ mind.

1	A where	B which	C that	D how
2	A widely	B widest	C wider	D wide
3	A take	B get	C see	D set
4	A those	B these	C them	D they
5	A in	B on	C by	D to

Summarize spoken text

In the test, there are 2–3 tasks. For each task, you listen to the audio then type your summary into the box on the screen. The wording in the instructions below is the same as you will see in the actual test. See page 45 for help.

You will hear a short lecture. Write a summary for a fellow student who was not present at the lecture. You should write 50–70 words.

10 min. You will have 10 minutes to finish this task. Your response will be judged on the quality of your writing and on how well your response presents the key points presented in the lecture.

1 ▸ 145

....

....

....

....

....

....

2 ▸ 146

....

....

....

....

....

....

Multiple-choice, choose multiple answers

In the test, there are 2–3 tasks. For each task, you listen to the audio then click the buttons next to all of the answers you think are correct. The wording in the instructions below is the same as you will see in the actual test. See page 47 for help.

Listen to the recording and answer the question by selecting all the correct responses. ***You will need to select more than one response.***

1 ▸ 147 **Which of these tips about doing a good translation does the speaker mention?**

- ○ A Always translate from a second language into your native language.
- ○ B Ask a native speaker if you are not sure of the meaning of something.
- ○ C Take care to choose the right meaning of a word if you use a dictionary.
- ○ D Don't translate technical texts unless you are familiar with the subject.
- ○ E Ask what your translation will be used for.

2 ▸ 148 **Which of these qualities of a building does the speaker mention as being important?**

- ○ A how attractive the building is to look at
- ○ B how original the design of the building is
- ○ C how well the building fits in with surrounding buildings
- ○ D how long the building is likely to last
- ○ E how well the building suits its purpose

Fill in the blanks

In the test, there are 2–3 tasks. For each task, there is a text with several gaps. You type the correct answer for each gap into the box in the text. The wording in the instructions below is the same as you will see in the actual test. See page 49 for help.

You will hear a recording. Type the missing words in each blank.

1 ▶ 149

I'd recommend that you all try to get hold of ***English in the Southern Hemisphere*** by Nolan and Watts, as this provides an excellent [1] ________ of the topics that we're going to be covering in this module. It's really our [2] ________ text. It has particularly strong sections on the history of English in Australia and New Zealand, examining in some depth how the language has [3] ________ in these countries. The sections on phonology and on vocabulary will be [4] ________ when you're doing the written assignment, which I'm going to be telling you about in a moment once I've given you the [5] ________ of a couple of other essential references.

2 ▶ 150

This week we're going to be continuing our discussion of women in society. Last week we looked at a number of [1] ________ relating to women in education. If you remember, we discussed women both at school and at university. Today we're going to be considering the [2] ________ that women play in the workplace. Again, we'll start by taking a historical perspective, and inevitably you'll find that many of the same [3] ________ that impacted on women in education also had a major influence on their working lives. In the second half of the lecture, I'll concentrate on the situation in [4] ________ today, and I'll invite you to suggest how you think things are likely to develop over the next [5] ________. OK, so let's get started.

Highlight correct summary

In the test, there are 2–3 tasks. For each task, you listen to the audio then click the button next to the summary you think is correct. The wording in the instructions below is the same as you will see in the actual test. See page 51 for help.

You will hear a recording. Click on the paragraph that best relates to the recording.

1 ▸ 151

- ○ A What makes people unique compared to other creatures is their hands. Their flexibility has allowed us to develop the manual skills that have made society what it is today. People should become more aware of the complicated anatomy of each of their hands.
- ○ B The thumb is the part of our hand which is most complicated in terms of the number of muscles which are required to control it. However, each of our fingers also depends on a set of nerves and muscles which enables it to carry out an extraordinary variety of different actions.
- ○ C The amazing flexibility of the human hand is truly remarkable. It is the result of a complex anatomy lying under the skin of the hand, and it can be useful to study this anatomy if you want to learn how to use your hands more effectively for sporting or other purposes.
- ○ D The human hand is extraordinarily flexible. It enables a person to do a remarkable variety of things, some demanding great precision and others requiring considerable strength. This is because of the complex structure of nerves, muscles and ligaments that makes up a hand.

You will hear a recording. Click on the paragraph that best relates to the recording.

❷ ▶ 152

○ A There are fewer Great White sharks in Australian waters than was once believed. This is because tagging has shown that sharks travel considerable distances, and a shark recorded east of Bass Strait one week is often recorded west of Bass Strait the next. However, sharks always return to their place of origin to breed.

○ B A recent research study has shown that Australian Great White shark populations have remained surprisingly distinct as, despite travelling long distances, these sharks do not breed away from their original areas. This means that local shark habitats may have a greater effect on sharks than has been believed up to now.

○ C There is a greater variety in the Great White shark populations in Australian waters than was previously thought to be the case. This means that some types of shark are actually more endangered than was believed. Scientists are therefore developing conservation programs which will help to protect these threatened species.

○ D An investigation of Great White sharks in Australian waters has come up with some unexpected conclusions, as it found that the genetic make-up of sharks in one area was quite distinct from those found elsewhere. This made scientists realize that sharks do not swim as far away from their home areas as used to be thought.

Multiple-choice, choose single answer

In the test, there are 2–3 tasks. For each task, you listen to the audio then click the button next to the answer you think is correct. The wording in the instructions below is the same as you will see in the actual test. See page 54 for help.

Listen to the recording and answer the multiple-choice question by selecting the correct response. *Only one response is correct.*

1 ▶ 153 **What point does the lecturer make about whales and sound pollution?**

- ○ A Increased sound pollution means whales 'talk' more at night than during the day.
- ○ B Research shows whales communicate to warn each other of sound pollution.
- ○ C Whales may not survive in some situations where there is sound pollution.
- ○ D Sound pollution from submarines has little impact on whales and other creatures.

2 ▶ 154 **What must the students do before next Wednesday?**

- ○ A email the slides for their presentation to the tutor
- ○ B make enough copies of their handouts
- ○ C post an outline of their talk to the course website
- ○ D practise giving their presentation

Select missing word

In the test, there are 2–3 tasks. For each task, you listen to the audio then click the button next to the words you think complete the audio. The wording in the instructions below is the same as you will see in the actual test. See page 56 for help.

1 ▶ 155 You will hear a recording about student assignments. *At the end of the recording the last word or group of words has been replaced by a beep.* Select the correct option to complete the recording.

- ○ A they made an inappropriate choice of topic
- ○ B they used illustrations and evidence well
- ○ C they showed they had grasped the content of the course
- ○ D they did not speak as clearly as they should have done

2 ▶ 156 You will hear a recording about poverty. *At the end of the recording the last word or group of words has been replaced by a beep.* Select the correct option to complete the recording.

- ○ A portraying those living conditions in a literary way
- ○ B bringing the situation to the attention of the public
- ○ C making use of their own experience of poverty
- ○ D helping the poor to gain a good education

Highlight incorrect words

In the test, there are 2–3 tasks. For each task, you listen to the audio and follow the words in the text on the screen. You click on the words that are different on the screen and the audio. The wording in the instructions below is the same as you will see in the actual test. See page 58 for help.

You will hear a recording. Below is a transcription of the recording. *Some words in the transcription differ from what the speaker said.* Please click on the words that are different.

1 ▶ 157 Transcription:

English had barely established itself as a language in England when it began spreading to other countries to be used there as well. First it passed north to Scotland and then west to Wales. It then made its path across the sea to Ireland. That was in the Middle Ages. Over the course of the following centuries it has put down roots all over the earth, from the USA to South Africa, from India to New Zealand. Of course, in all these places it has developed in special ways to suit the new concepts in which it found itself.

2 ▶ 158 Transcription:

Researchers at the University of California claim to have discovered that people who eat chocolate regularly tend to be lighter than those who hardly eat it. The findings may seem suspicious in that chocolate has a great many calories and, in general, the more calories people contain, the more likely they are to put on weight. The recent studies establish that it is more the regularity with which people eat chocolate that is important rather than the amount they consume. Whether they eat a little or a lot seems to make no difference, whereas eating it freely appears to reduce weight more than only having it occasionally.

Write from dictation

In the test, there are 3–4 tasks. For each task, you listen and type the sentence you hear into the box on the screen. The wording in the instructions below is the same as you will see in the actual test. See page 60 for help.

You will hear a sentence. Type the sentence in the box below exactly as you hear it. Write as much of the sentence as you can. You will hear the sentence only once.

1 ▶ 159

....

....

....

2 ▶ 160

....

....

....

3 ▶ 161

....

....

....